ETHICS IN ACTION

Tang Chun-I Lecture Series

The Tang Chun-I Lecture Series is based on lectures and seminars delivered by distinguished scholars who are holding the Tang Chun-I Visiting Professorship at The Chinese University of Hong Kong. This professorship was initiated in 2003 by the Department of Philosophy, The Chinese University of Hong Kong, in memory of the late Professor Tang Chun-I (1909–1978), a major figure in twentieth-century Chinese philosophy and the first Chair Professor of the Department of Philosophy.

The Tang Chun-I Lecture Series III

Ethics in Action

Workable Guidelines for Public and Private Choices

Donald J. Munro

The Chinese University Press

Ethics in Action: Workable Guidelines for Public and Private Choices
By Donald J. Munro

ISBN 978-962-996-380-4

THE CHINESE UNIVERSITY PRESS
The Chinese University of Hong Kong
SHA TIN, N.T., HONG KONG
Fax: +852 2603 6692
+852 2603 7355
E-mail: cup@cuhk.edu.hk
Web-site: www.chineseupress.com

Printed in Hong Kong

Contents

Preface

There are quite a few reasons why I took the trouble to do the research for a graduate seminar and some public lectures at The Chinese University of Hong Kong (CUHK). I wanted to repay the honor I received from the Philosophy Department when they invited me to be a Tang Chun-I (Tang Junyi) Visiting Professor in 2006. But I had other motives for the direction those studies took.

Probing the assumptions in various schools and fields about human nature, and the practical implications of those assumptions, has been an enduring interest. This is especially true of my links to certain Chinese thinkers. Nowadays the topics of human nature and of the mind are widely studied in the sciences, such as the cognitive neurosciences and evolutionary psychology. So, in order to bring myself up to date, for a number of years I have joined faculty seminars at Michigan that discuss those developments. I note with thanks the Evolution and Human Adaptation Program, led by Randolph Nesse M.D. These matters, I felt, would be of interest to my audience at the Chinese University. Another motive involves political opinions, personal experiences, and the Confucian ideal of *zhi xing heyi* (the unity of knowledge and action). This refers to the practical application of some ethical principles to social policies.

My close friend and college roommate, Robert A. G. Monks, has been a corporate CEO, director of corporations, lawyer, and the head of the U.S. government's agency that monitors the nation's pension systems. In those stylishly appointed suites where he worked, he learned that short-term efficiency and material profit often are the only signs of success that concern corporate executives and their boards of trustees. Believing that the public good and the interests of shareholder owners have been ignored when such a standard is employed, he insisted that there are other factors to be added to the indicators of success or failure. By focusing on corporate governance (especially on relations between boards and executive officers, and on matters of transparency) he has tried to increase the voice of shareholders. They are the real owners of the companies and lasting guardians of their futures. I was moved by his accounts of both the difficulties he has faced and also his many rewards in providing the necessary services and clout to those seeking governance change. These include founding the very successful Institutional Shareholder Services and The Corporate Library.[1]

At the same time that I was learning about these matters, I was getting involved with a political action group, The Interfaith Partnership for Political Action (IPPA, www.InterfaithPoliticalAction .org; see Part Three of this book). Coming from different religious or secular backgrounds, the founders (including me) started by agreeing that the short-term profit standard or economic model was pervasive in our culture. We agreed that the then current administration in Washington had placed true believers in a narrow idea of the economic model into the highest departmental and oversight offices. The IPPA members went on to agree on the following different position: "Policies rooted in our shared human principles serve us better than policies based only on a purely economic model that says material success alone is the best measure of human happiness and well being.... We favor using moral guidance to inform the standard economic model." The best political polices are those that can be justified economically *and* ethically. The latter strengthens any argument made on only economic grounds.

Mr. Monks has written convincingly about the negative social consequences of relying only on the standard economic model. But what I felt had not been adequately put forth anywhere was the *content* of a moral standard that could guide questions about the right thing to do in many public and private choices. It is easy for a presidential candidate to say that "there is a moral imperative to ensure that quality affordable health care is available to all Americans." But most of them never tell us what the content of such a moral standard is. To try filling the gap, I chose the subject matter that I delivered in those presentations at CUHK and, then, in this book.

By drawing on findings in the cognitive sciences and evolutionary psychology, I can go on to say why I think certain ethical principles help us as humans to succeed biologically as individuals and as cooperative groups. Examples that will appear in the book are: sympathy, reciprocity, foresight, consistency, fairness, trust, respect or honor, and model emulation. Underlying our exercise of all of them is my belief in the equal worth of all human lives. Whether these principles are present or absent in a family, large group, or organization can provide us with additional considerations when measuring success and failure.

Let me illustrate with the concrete period in our human history in which we now live. In the United States, for many widely read opinion makers as well as for many corporations, in measuring profit/loss, global warming and pollution have been mere "externalities," not entered into the ledger. Even the most environmentally sophisticated spokesmen continue to rely on the old economic model. Here is *The New York Times* writer Thomas Friedman on the greening of geopolitics:

> The only way we are going to get innovations that drive energy costs down to the China price [the price China would pay for coal-fired energy today]—innovations in energy-saving appliances, lights, and building materials and in non–CO_2-emitting power plants and fuels—is by mobilizing free-market capitalism. The only thing as powerful as Mother Nature is Father Greed. To a degree, the market is already at work on this project—because some venture capitalists and companies understand that clean-tech is going to be the next great global industry.[2]

What is missing here is the ethical argument and the incentive ordinary people may have for changing their consumer habits and wishes. For example, recycling is widely practiced in our country on a voluntary basis. Occasionally voters vote it down because of the costs paid for by taxes. Even those costs are rapidly falling, as a market grows for our paper, cardboard, and tin. But overall, recycling has a grass roots basis. People do it because they think it is the right thing. This can apply also to dealing with the problem of carbon emissions. The Friedman position ignores that power of figuring that something is right and then doing it. In the first section of Part Two, where I discuss moral complexities in choices about global warming, I explain what is missing when, faced with dangerous carbon emissions, people put all their expectations in Father Greed's hands. Absent: the ethical principle of equal human worth (highlighted in the United States in "all men are created equal," and in the United Nations Universal Declaration of Human Rights). Treating people equally is honored in the practices of those who advocate universal health care. To neglect measures to reduce carbon emissions is to accept likely damage to the healthy lives of children and grandchildren. So the argument for backing what is clean and green can be both money from innovations and also treating current and future generations as if their healthy lives have equal worth.

I use trust and consistency as an example of two related ethical principles. Trust is a prominent topic these days. In the United States, writers have described how CEOs and their boards legally destroy trust in their organizations, relying on regulations affirmed by friendly representatives in congress or in the oversight agencies. For example, they do so by transferring risk away from the corporations and on to employees, when they terminate pension plans and shift workers to a "defined contribution plan." The real benefits come to the financial services industry that will manage those savings accounts. In my own book here I try to explain what trust and consistency involve and how they strengthen a social group. I also deal with our basic quest for respect or honor, and avoidance of shame. When leaders do the right or wrong thing, public honor or shame are powerful incentives, inadequately used in the United States.

I take the ethical guidelines from Part One, and apply them primarily to China in Part Two. The global warming topic is there because both China and the United States have been pointing fingers at each other for years, unwilling to make any serious moves on the carbon problem unless the other side does. But the comments are relevant to many countries, not simply to China. As for the other application topic, the search for consistency in the Chinese legal system, it is there because China wants to regard itself as modern. It copies many good and bad American traits in the search. In this connection, its treatment of the law is a mixed bag. Unfortunately China's authoritarian political style involves traditional, not modern Western attitudes toward the law. Meanwhile step by step the implementation of desirable legal institutions continues. The rule of law, prized in the United States, requires some consistency in its application. The Chinese authorities have not adequately dealt with the power of local officials to interpret the law in their towns or counties as they wish, and for their own monetary advantages.

In doing research for the lectures and graduate seminar presented in 2006, I had a final motive. It was to show my respect for members of the Philosophy Department at CUHK and to Tang Junyi and his legacy. This is the subject of a conversation in Part Three with Professor Cheung Chan-fai. There is another conversation there with Professor Liu Xiaogan, where I try to answer some challenges and criticisms thrown my way by Liu and other reviewers.

My special thanks to the tough critics who have nailed me at various points in the writing of this material, causing me to see the light and revise. I owe a special debt to Chad Hansen, Ann Munro, An Yanming, and Joanne Reuss. I am also grateful to these kin who corrected many dark spots in my writing: Diana Medalie, Cynthia Beeker, Elisabeth Smith, and Eleanor Munro. Chad Hansen helped me clarify what a workable ethics would be, including some of the words to describe it.

Professor Donald J. Munro

Front row from left: Professor Kwan Tze-wan, Professor Daniel Law, Professor Donald J. Munro, Mrs. Munro, Professor Jack C. Y. Cheng, Professor Cheung Chan-fai. Back row from left: Professor Leung Ka-wing, Professor Lau Kwok-keung, Professor Yao Zhihua, Professor Lau Chong-fuk, Professor Florence Chan, Professor Chong Kim-chong, Professor Wong Kai-yee, Professor Lin Hui, Dr. Kou Kei-chun, Mr. Cheng Shun-cheong

1

The Standard and the Guidelines

The Evolutionary Basis of the Five Moral Intuitions

Introduction

In securing stability for a society and in socializing children, authorities often, and sometimes justifiably, resort to fear of punishment and control of the purse to get their ways. But fear and the money incentive also are often misused, with suffering in store for the populace or children who are their targets. Examples are commonplace, such as Stalin's gulags and their subsequent condemnation, and parental child abuse leading to laws about foster care for young victims. The misuse of fear and the purse is why people also have sought to rediscover and reassert an additional source for compliance with the goals of leaders, parents, and teachers. Deeply embedded in human history, this other is a standard of values or of moral guidelines. In short, it facilitates knowing the right thing and, with commitment, easily doing it. In so doing, having a standard can alter the roles of fear and of control by an economic system in maintaining social order.

Possession of muscle by the authority does not make a goal or policy right. Metaphorically, a kind of social contract exists in large societies and in large organizations, in that normally people act so as to sustain social harmony. Fear and monetary reward play a part. But people's motives are mixed. They may act both to avoid punishment and to earn a profit, and also believe that what they do is right or wrong. With commitment to moral guidelines comes a motive to act other than fear or profit. As early Confucians knew long ago, and as Western social scientists learned more recently, when there is acceptance of a moral standard, the probability for compliance increases even when the symbol of punishment (the military, guards, police) are not around. The lawmaker is inside the people's minds. So there is a difference between fear and profit, transitory causes of human choices, and being aware of virtuous models or ideal codes of conduct that provide standards for right and wrong.

Recently, politicians in the United States have said things to the effect that there is a moral imperative to ensure that every single American has quality affordable health coverage, or that global warming is not just an economic issue but also is a moral issue. Exxon Mobile has been publicly criticized for a single-minded focus on economic matters. But, routinely, the advocates of adding the moral perspective never tell us what the content of that moral standard is. In the following paragraphs, I lay out what such a content can look like. It has room for both self-interest and cooperative behavior, for some of the way things are, and also the way they should be. I show the distinction between what is instinctive in our desires and what is partly learned. The former is based in biology. The latter, rooted in instincts but also containing beliefs and emotions influenced by where we are born and live, I call moral intuitions. They will be central to the content of the moral standard.

Given the right conditions, for example, cooperation and the public good can assert themselves as goals over short-term individual or corporate profit or fear. Those conditions include the sharing of information about who is and is not contributing to the group good, including information about cheaters who take and do not give. Sometimes we are all in groups in which cooperation is almost an unavoidable option, as when our countries face a genuine enemy threat. Often it is just the most beneficial choice. The right conditions also include the availability of information about people's reputations, length of relationships, promises and threats, enforcement agencies, and opportunities to use information to select cooperation partners.[1] The conditions also include political or social stability, available life sustaining resources, and degree of cultural assimilation or homogeneity. The assimilation or homogeneity can come about in part because of people's shared cultural experiences and learning in schools. Shared perspectives can be strengthened by central government mandates about educational content. Or, in a given society, cultural balkanization and even technology such as the Internet can challenge homogeneity of values. In any case, the goals of cooperative efforts still need to be spelled out for individuals and groups.

I am a non-traditional utilitarian who treats securing joy and the avoidance of suffering as pretty basic real-life human motives. I still hold that appealing to a moral standard in choices fits right into real-life situations involving pain and pleasure. This is because the shame and honor that usually accompany making morally bad or good choices can be the source of life-time pain or pleasure. But there is much more to a moral system than just joy and suffering. So I now turn to the content of workable moral guidelines and where they come from.

A main goal of the sections that follow is to show the relevance to ethics of hypotheses about human nature in the sciences. This is especially true of the findings and interpretations of the cognitive sciences, evolutionary biology, and evolutionary psychology.[2] Because they concern patterns of social behavior, emotions, and intuitions, these works, along with culture studies, explain some of the social behavior that can be expected of most of us. The findings also suggest what ethical guidelines will likely work. I stress the relevance and suggestions for ethics of the scientific findings as revealed in the psychological and biological literature. I do not refer to their scientific accuracy or probabilities. That is for scientists themselves to do.

Philosophers would describe "working" as "ought should imply can," meaning something becomes a legitimate duty only if we *can* perform it. What ought to be done should not put highly unreasonable demands on the subject's ordinary motives and attitudes. The findings of science about human nature become relevant when they are linked to a moral system. As I use the term, a moral system is an ideal code of conduct that provides a standard for judging right and wrong. In this section, its authority derives from intuitions (individual conscience) derived in part from human biology. The field that studies it is meta-ethics. In this work, its theoretical basis is what I call two-realm utilitarianism, a type of ethical naturalism.

A moral system that works is natural in the sense that it *takes account of human motives and predispositions* that have their origins in biology; in theory they may be explained in terms of their evolutionary function for humans or related primates. Also, a natural moral system promotes human solidarity with a minimum of *coercion* and a maximum of *autonomous compliance*, compliance even when no symbol of coercion is present. This is one reason why such a system can work. When there is a correspondence between, on the one hand, what we believe is right, and, on the other hand, some of our naturally strong desires (I will call them "ultimate desires"), doing the right thing can run from being smooth to almost automatic. Such a moral system is also pluralistic in that it derives from different cultures and is limited by our existing motives and attitudes. Nature limits all cultural moralities and positively favors and facilitates some of them.

At this time in history, in both China and the United States, the most prominent standard for defining good/bad policy, or success/failure is the economic one (efficient/wasteful, material profit/loss). While deserving attention, this standard alone ignores whether a policy, idea, or product is beneficial or not to the public, particularly taking a long-term perspective. I believe that proposals for most new policies are stronger when citizens and political leaders understand and can state whether this public benefit exists or not. Often a case can be made for a choice affecting the public that satisfies both an economic need and an ethical principle. An example is innovations in green technology that lead to both saleable products and a positive impact on climate change. The latter, concerning the health and lives of people, has ethical implications. In my own country, voters should be aware of the claimed non-economic benefits, and politicians should expect to take a stand on them. A workable moral system is a source for considerations about such benefits, for individuals and for the public. To help identify a workable standard, and then apply it, is the reason for this essay.

Evolutionary psychology is primarily about minds and is only secondarily about genes. It explores beliefs, desires, motives, emotions, and intuitions, and the social behavior with which they are associated. Researchers in the field are more concerned with how we humans are similar, rather than how we differ. Cultural psychologists also study minds and contribute to our knowledge of them. Behavioral genetics deals with our differences. In studying the mind, evolutionary psychologists try to determine how the various emotions, motives, and other psychological activities are adaptive. Do they play a role in the process of natural selection, and if so what?

Psychologists call these the "proximate mechanisms" that lead an individual to certain behavior, such as altruism or joining groups. They are concerned with both negative actions and feelings (aggression, deception, hate) and positive ones (sympathy, love, trust). As tools, researchers use functional magnetic resonance imaging (fMRI) and positron-emission tomography (PET). They also study levels of hormones and neurotransmitters (cortisol, oxytocin, serotonin, dopamine), cultural variables, damage to the brain, and primate behavior.

A weakness in the field of evolutionary psychology is that few practitioners attempt to apply their findings and theories to urgent social problems, such as climate change, large economic inequalities, and cronyism in law and government. Yet I believe that their findings are particularly relevant to the ethical principles suggested by such problems. Those principles suggest imperatives for certain identifiable choices. In the second part of this work I will explore two social problems in China (global warming, and defects in the legal system). I will show how the ethical issues mandate certain specific choices.

There is nothing inherently good or bad about the beliefs, desires, motives, and emotions and behaviors anchored in evolution. We are born with tendencies or instincts toward sympathy and altruism, as well as toward tribalism and dividing into in-groups and out-groups. Evolution uses survival and reproductive fitness as standards for "success" for individuals and for groups.

> *Kin selection* [among genetic relatives, as understood in the evolutionary process] is the natural selection of genes based on their effects on individuals carrying them plus the effects the presence of the genes has on all the genetic relatives of the individual ... who still live and are capable either of reproducing or of affecting the reproduction of blood relatives. Kin selection is especially important in the origin of altruistic behavior.[3]

The roots of tribalism lie in the initial tendency of humans to seek fitness only for themselves and for their genetic kin ("inclusive fitness").[4] Tribalism draws boundaries around the kin group and other in-groups. But tribalism goes beyond the kinship group to include non-kin who share such traits as territory, appearance, language, and religion/culture. Typically, members also share an imagined community based on stories of their common past.[5] In

China, these would include the stories of Yu, who controlled flooding, and of the Yellow Emperor.

The instincts of sympathy and altruism can be overcome by patriotism or ideology. When a country is attacked, for example, tribal patriotism is useful for uniting its people in defense. Demonstrating the dangers of ideology, Leninist and Maoist leaders attempted to replace sympathy and altruism with a concern only for members of certain designated revolutionary classes.[6] Add to this the widespread fear of state punishment, and it is easy to see why a particular population may seem to repudiate altruism in favor of conformity to a state teaching. But as a counterforce, the intellect and the emotions can be used to blunt the inclination to put tribal welfare first. Jonathan Glover reports that early in his administration, John F. Kennedy and several members of his cabinet (McNamara, Rusk) spent an afternoon being briefed on the full consequences of nuclear war. This struck emotionally at their existing values. These officials were among the doves opposing a nuclear attack on Cuba. Dean Rusk said that a sudden air strike "had no support in law or morality."[7]

Humans have mixed motives. Their reasons for selecting friends, or groups in which to cooperate, vary. They often include the material resources the others can bestow on them or displays of wealth that they then can copy themselves. This is the economic market or, perhaps, the patronage system model.[8] But what is special about humans is our ability to have other motives that trump social selection on the basis of being resource-rich. As the main force in such choices, people may instead follow the personality or moral character of others, or shared interests of others. There is something reductive about the social selection psychologists who stress that people display for public-relation purposes their moral characters in much the way they do their cars, property, and bank accounts. Some of the time, perhaps, but not most of the people most of the time. Randolph Nesse says:

> Reputation display competitions may be important for explaining human moral capacities and altruistic behaviors that are not reciprocated.[9]

This is a very narrow account of why people do the right thing. They may actually prize a value such as sympathy as well as feel it, and practice it with no public-relations concern present at all.

Hence we need an ethical standard by which we can determine which intuitions and behavioral tendencies are desirable and should be cultivated, and which ones are potentially dangerous. As Steven Pinker puts it, "The facts [about human nature] must be combined with a statement of values and a method of resolving conflicts among them."[10] I will now turn to the standard I advocate and the values that follow from it.

From Two-Realm Utilitarianism to the Five Intuitions

I can agree with traditional utilitarianism that actions should be judged by their consequences. And consequences have something to do with happiness, or with joy and suffering. Two-realm utilitarianism maintains that for any individual, there are two groups with whose happiness she should be concerned. One is all humans; the other is close relatives, neighbors, and communities with whom she bonds. And she has different duties to each of those groups. In terms of her own resources and care, she may be partial toward her own family members, because of the strength of emotional bonds to them. At the same time, she should treat as sacred the impartial laws, domestic and international, that provide protection and nurturance to those physically distant and unknown to her and that foster their happiness. These are positive laws that also conform to moral laws that derive from the equal worth of all persons (see below) and promote joy and minimize suffering. I make the assumption that the laws to which I refer are legitimate and are worthy of our respect as sacred. They are legitimate when legislated by representatives of the people, without coercion, and by a body of legislators that retains its power against other parts of a government. It also requires that voters and legislators recognize that all people share in having the same moral intuitions ("we hold these truths to be self-evident") or ultimate desires. Happiness and joy/suffering refer to our overall sense of well-being—our experience of satisfying or not satisfying, what some call the ultimate desires (later I will describe five such ultimate desires).

There are two moral realms to which we have different degrees of concern. One is ordered by "public morality," with rules that promote the joy and minimize the suffering of all persons. The other is the realm of "private morality" and private choices. Public morality requires obeying laws, and, as one's motivation permits, private charity.

Private morality accepts the equal worth of all persons. But, in addition, it has another standard of the worth of persons that coexists in tension with the idea of equal worth. I cannot agree with the traditional utilitarian notion that humans should always strive for "the greatest happiness of the greatest number." Our inborn emotions do not provide most of us with the motivation to care much for people we neither know nor, because of physical or other separation, can do much to help. We have stronger private obligations for family and local community. This is a potential weakness in traditional utilitarianism. Even J. S. Mill admitted that in most individuals, the feeling of equal regard for all is "much inferior in strength to their selfish feelings."[11] I interpret this position as lending support to my own two-realm view. Both realms (equal regard for all, and the selfish feeling) are legitimate in taking account of evolutionary-based motives and predispositions. Our choices often concern how to weigh and balance them. Among other things, this involves learning how all people share the same ultimate desires, and what the consequences are of satisfying them or not. Humans are capable of cooperation, or acting on behalf of a common good that conflicts with some short-term personal pleasure. The law provides the muscle for some of those choices.

Because of certain shared human traits, we should presume that there are some grounds for the idea that people have equal worth. Five such traits are particularly striking. One is shared DNA. About 99% of human DNA is the same, though important differences among us can still exist due to the remaining non-similar part. The second is the ability to feel joy and suffering (which I regard as ethically the most important trait) and the ability to express these, and other feelings, in language. As Antonio Damasio has said, the body seeks to preserve itself, and joy/suffering are clues to its status in that matter.[12] Third, there is the experience of being loved by another person, or the desire to be loved. Fourth, there are the shared moral intuitions. For example, all humans share an ability to foresee consequences, to plan and choose accordingly, along with a desire to control our choices and resulting actions. In the West, this process is often called autonomy. Or, we have an ability to judge equality/inequality in social relations and to find a response fair or unfair. Consider human language as a fifth trait, useful in making reference to some of the feelings and intuitions. At certain times in Western history, other traits were cited as the basis of equality of worth, such as having souls created in God's image, or being equally loved by God.

Our awareness of these universal traits provides a strong argument to value all humans as equals and to consider carefully how we treat one another. This is the basis for "equal treatment before the law," a principle cited over the entrance to the U.S. Supreme Court building. Equal worth based on shared traits justifies equal treatment under the law, domestic and international. Thus, in public morality, equal worth is also derived from legitimate legal statutes. They contribute to the utilitarian goal of general happiness for all humans. Because the magnitude of compassion people will have for those beyond the family is variable and unpredictable, *impartial laws and rules of conduct* are required to provide protection and nurturance to those not well known to the individual choice maker. Just as our innate compassion may lead us to acts of charity, we are also subject to laws and moral rules that benefit us and others. An example would be the laws that protect us against our rulers, embodied in the division of powers and in the oversight agencies within governmental departments. So, "consequences" in the public realm are the ways in which certain policies or laws promote the greatest happiness.

Impartiality and Partiality

Impartiality, sometimes spoken of as neutrality, is often a virtue. It promotes attention to a wide range of facts and encourages competition among theories and proposed solutions to problems. However, when used in ethics as opposed to law or science, impartiality can be limiting. An impartial observer is often locked into an emotionally neutral, overly detached, or passive stance.[13] To be disinterested is likely to be devoid of the emotional engagement that motivates much moral action. With this perspective, many have argued that judicial nominees should be required to have some real-life experiences.

In his book *Moral Minds*, the biologist Marc Hauser, influenced by John Rawls, treats impartiality as central to how we make moral judgments. Rawls says that in thinking about justice, we must operate under a *veil of ignorance.* As Hauser interprets this, we cannot think about anyone's personal characteristics, including relationships. In his view, these are morally irrelevant biases. Hauser says:

> In terms of a general theory of morality, we want to exclude possible biases that may cause us to see as just situations that favor the in-group over the out-group; I use the notion of "exclude" here as a practical desideratum, acknowledging upfront that we inherited from our primate cousins (and probably before) a highly partial and biased mind-set, one designed initially to favor kin. It is this in-group bias that must be overcome if we are to advance an impartial moral theory.[14]

Frankly, I am shocked that a thoughtful person could ignore the moral relevance of our most powerful emotions, those that bind us to our kin. For Hauser, the term "impartial" trumps other considerations. Hauser's treatment of the problem of when to end life-support is an example. He does show the inadequacy of consulting only the monetary consequences.[15] This means there are non-monetary considerations or other consequences that count. But does this not open the door for some allowance of partiality? In my view, decisions about special care normally should be the responsibility of kin and their resources. Potentially there will always be conflicts between the law, which favors impartiality, and social norms that permit us to favor kin. Finally, as for the quotation, Rawls does in fact have a full-information component (knowing social contexts for our choices). Also, he was designing principles of justice, not morality.

Assuming the value of impartiality, and also searching for principles underlying our judgments of permissible harm to others, Hauser uses the well-known tests in which respondents are asked what to do in the case of an out-of-control trolley. The conductor has been suddenly disabled. A commuter standing nearby can choose to let the trolley continue on the track, where five or six people are standing a short way forward. Or, he can turn the trolley onto a side track, where there are fewer people standing, unaware of the trolley. Those being tested are not allowed to ask if those on the side track are related to the commuter. In effect the testers strip the participants of their ability to consider the emotional dimensions of the scenario by never letting them know if the potential victims are kin, neighbors, or friends.[16]

I advocate looking at people not only from the standpoint of equal treatment under the law, but also from the perspective of our strongest and most enduring emotions. Based on my emotions, people are of unequal worth. The lives of my family and community members are worth more to me than those of outsiders. So their joy and suffering, which are signs of the well-being of their lives, are more worthy of my concerns. This means I have special obligations to them in terms of my own resources and care.

There is a difference between public morality and the individual's own private standard or attitude. Because I am interested in workable ethics, I care about what motivates action. And I believe that motivation comes primarily from emotional commitment, and secondarily from beliefs in the utility of legal rules. That emotional commitment varies depending on a person's feelings toward the object. Those emotions, in particular love, bestow worth to varying degrees.

As Chad Hansen has argued,[17] the rules of public morality should include each person taking care of those closest to him or her. A rule utilitarian could argue that requiring individuals to care for their own is the most efficient way to achieve general happiness for all. This assumption is consistent with the general utilitarian standard. However, for me, I will act on behalf of my own not primarily because I want to follow a rule, but because I am motivated by my unequal love for my own in comparison with my love for others.

This contrasts with the general utilitarian position, which assigns equal value to all, regardless of our emotional attachments. The affirmation of equal value is also the public stance of the Bill and Melinda Gates Foundation, whose website declares: "All lives—no matter where they are being led—have equal value." This is a position to which I also adhere, but which I treat as the realm for duties derived from legitimate law, with other motives to be derived from personal feelings manifest in charity. The general utilitarian support for a single-realm utilitarianism is that the value of humans should not be dependent on our actual feelings. Otherwise, egocentric psychopaths (Stalin) would have no duties, and selfless altruists (Mother Theresa) would not act in ways that transcend their egos. My first reply is that psychopaths do have moral and legal duties not to obstruct the rights of others, and should be held accountable. My second is that the selfless altruist is an exception to the ordinary. Just as the phenomenon of color-blindness does not keep us from describing certain visual experiences as "normal," so the existence of selfless altruists will not stop me from saying that most people most of the time, will find Mother Theresa's style of selflessness very difficult. As Steven Pinker has noted, her style also involved rather limited and ascetic care. Most people will find it easier to act on the preferential feelings they have for kin and those who share community ties. This, in turn, is relevant to what works in ethics. Certainly, in the abstract, the Mother Theresa model is noble. But we will still find the bioethicist Peter Singer asking how the Gates family can justify on the one hand, believing in equal worth and giving away US$30 billion, and, on the other hand, living in a US$100 million house.[18] At least in the short term the answer is preferential concern for family, as one among their competing ordinary and legitimate emotions and motives.

So, in addition to the public realm of impartial laws and rules of conduct, there is a place for household guidelines for family and community members, incorporating preferential treatment of kin. These guidelines apply primarily to allocations of time, care, and financial resources. "Consequences" refers to events or actions that promote the special happiness of all members of a family and/or community. "Community" also includes bonds to which we are likely to apply family terminology within non-kinship organizations. An example would be the "bands of brothers" whose enduring bonds stem from shared experiences within the military. Normally, only strong emotion leads an individual to take action that results in major useful consequences. I am most likely to want to help those who are physically close to me; therefore special standards govern my behavior toward them. This is one reason that photography and other arts play a valuable role in stirring my emotions toward those physically distant from me, whose moral worth I experience less strongly.

To sum up, the two-realm utilitarian will ask what the *consequences* are that result from good laws, or from family and community oriented choices. She is not only interested in material cost/benefit. In order to flag what are morally relevant consequences, I will identify from the scientific literature desires that are most likely to maximize the participants' senses of well being.

Human Instincts and the Five Ultimate Desires

"Consequences" of concern in the standard I am describing are those events in the public and private domains that satisfy some of the ultimate desires. These consequences promote happiness. The desires begin in the realm of instincts. Evolutionary biologists and psychologists use the expression *proximate mechanisms* to refer to tendencies that arise through natural selection. Here I call them instincts, and they refer to inborn patterns of responses to certain stimuli or situations. A review of standard sources in these fields finds four fundamental instincts shared by all humans.

One is *parental care for offspring and genetic kin.* That is, mother-infant bonding and kin selection.[19] A second is the *avoidance of bodily injury*, a response to signals of tissue damage. Elliott Sober and David Sloan Wilson say, "Pain is typically associated with bodily injury. Present day organisms seek to avoid pain, because this strategy was favored by natural selection."[20] Antonio Damasio describes "the body sensing regions [that] produce a precise map of what is occurring in the body," including the pathways that convey tissue damage.[21] The third is altruistic behavior in the form of *reciprocity and sharing.* As Robert Trivers puts it:

> [G]iven the universal and nearly daily practice of reciprocal altruism among humans today, it is reasonable to assume that it has been an important factor in recent human evolution and that the underlying emotional dispositions affecting altruistic behavior have important genetic components.[22]

Reciprocity is basic to cooperation, on which individual and group cooperation depend. Finally, there is action (such as downcast eyes and low posture, or the reverse) according to *status in a hierarchy.* Status is found in all complex mammalian societies and is often correlated with genetic fitness.

From these basic biological instincts, humans have developed a set of *moral intuitions.* Some people in certain contexts refer to them as values. Drawing a term from Elliott Sober and David Sloan Wilson, I will also call them "ultimate desires."[23] "Ultimate desires" is a richer term than intuitions, which some treat as pertaining only to items of knowledge. These five desires, common to all humans and rooted in evolution, provide motivation and moral basis for the choices we make in life. There is a large instinctive component to these desires, along with emotions and non-instinctive cognitive beliefs about how to satisfy them. When we make moral choices, we normally think in terms of these intuitions and the consequences that follow from acting on them. We do not necessarily think in terms of the joy or suffering with which those ultimate desires are instinctively linked.

To refer to five ultimate human desires is not to say that they are present to the same degree in every individual. There is plasticity in the neural pathways in the brain, variation in the pathways used by neurotransmitters, and different versions of the same genetic sequence. This opens the door to differences of personality. Many feel sympathy and empathy for other humans. Some, including certain autistic people and socio-paths, range from asocial to anti-social. But normally, people display some form of sympathy. There is promising work that suggests it may be rooted in the mirror neurons discovered in 1992 by a team led by the Italian neuroscientist Giacomo Rizzolatti.[24]

The first of the five ultimate desires is for *health and well-being of the body*. In Damasio's words:

> We happen to be biologically structured in a certain way—mandated to survive and to maximize pleasurable rather than painful survival....[25]

Following Damasio, I would define well-being in terms of joy and suffering.

The second ultimate desire is *love* between infant and caregiver, and, by extension, for close kin. It includes *the desire to be loved.* This love is linked to *sympathy*, or the capacity to be moved by events in the lives of others. *Empathy* is also involved, and strictly speaking it includes experiencing vicariously what another person feels. Thus in empathy there is a cognitive addition to sympathy, as we think about what another person thinks and feels.[26]

This desire is also basic to the origin of altruism.[27] If reproductive fitness is the evolutionary basis for altruism, then a proximate cause would be sympathy. "Mirror neurons" play a role here, as they facilitate our immediate grasp of the inner activities of the minds of other persons. Mirror neurons are subsets of neurons in the brains of humans and monkeys that react when an individual performs a certain act, or when he looks at another individual doing the same act. They give the observer an immediate internal comprehension of the other individual's inner experience, including intention and emotion. This is similar to what European phenomenologists refer to when they say that to understand something one must experience it, or empathically know it.

The third ultimate desire is for *fairness*, which is linked to empathy, equality, and *reciprocity* in exchanges.[28] It is also bound up with *trust*, in that the sense of fairness involves trust that all relevant parties will be treated according the rules of reciprocity. As with other desires, this can conflict with tribal instincts. Marc Hauser has found that all societies have a sense of fairness, though they differ in their views of what constitutes inequity. He also proposes that our innate ability to do numbers is related to our ability to think in terms of the equality of exchanges. Reciprocity also involves the ability to calculate costs and benefits, and to remember them so as to punish cheaters.[29] Equality as fairness can coexist with differences in quantities of goods exchanged, as a function of culturally socialized emotions about what is an equal share. In the business world, this might apply to the percentage of difference between executive and hourly salaries that are considered fair. In our autonomous choices, we ourselves also contribute to the judgment of what is fair and equal.

Fairness is not necessarily the same as impartiality. While advocating impartiality in the law, I criticize it in private morality, where I recognize the coexistence of fairness and unequal worth.

Respect or Esteem is the fourth ultimate desire. Derived from our experience in societal hierarchies, it is manifest in our prizing of respect and dignity and in our aversion to shame. The human desire for respect and avoidance of shame serve as a control mechanism by which groups encourage conformity and cooperation. I will discuss these in more detail later in this section, and also in Part Two, "Applications."

The final desire is for a combination of *foresight* about the consequences of our acts and of *control* over our resulting choices. This derives from the instinct to avoid injury, achieved by being alert to good and bad choices, and by the ability to come up with creative responses to danger. At the private level, our value of autonomy derives from this desire and also plays a role in human self-preservation. In Damasio's words:

> Eventually, in a fruitful combination with past memories, imagination, and reasoning, feelings led to the emergence of foresight and the possibility of creating novel, non stereotypical responses.[30]

Choosing is a known neural process. The Italian neuroscientists who first discovered the mirror neurons, write as follows about the evolutionary advantage that comes from understanding or foreseeing the intent of others:

> Given that humans and monkeys are social species, it is not difficult to see the potential survival advantage of a mechanism, based on mirror neurons ... permitting the direct and immediate comprehension of others' behavior without complex cognitive machinery. In social life, however, understanding others' emotion is equally important. Indeed, emotion is often a key contextual element that signals the intent of an action. That is why we and other research groups have also been exploring whether the mirror system allows us to understand what others feel in addition to what they do.[31]

We can choose our own actions based in part on how we predict other people will react to our acts. At the group and individual level, foresight is associated with the value of consistency in public or in private conduct. Consistency allows predictability, which promotes cooperation.

Marc Hauser stresses that moral systems depend on "forward-looking individuals who can bypass, for self and other, the temptation to feed immediate self-interest." Cooperative and stable social relationships require foresight:

> And in humans, at least, these social relations often depend upon the development of a rich sense of self, empathic concern for others, and the ability to generate predictions about others' states of mind without any direct experience of their behavior.[32]

Thus the "consequences" that are most relevant to two-realm utilitarianism are the fulfillment/neglect of the ultimate desires, often as a result of people following policies or laws (public realm) and household guidelines (private realm). Ignoring those desires and the two-realm standard leads to serious negative consequences for societies and individuals. One common error by politicians, and social engineers is to ignore the prominence of the nuclear family and of the meaning of community contact. One example is the Maoist attempt in the early 1960s to substitute communal dining halls for family kitchens. This policy dramatically failed, as the rural population hated it, and compliance dwindled.

To sum up, we have inborn patterns of response (instincts) to certain stimuli. These are the origins of our moral intuitions, which play out on emotional, cognitive, and motivational levels. I identify five such moral intuitions as ultimate desires. Their satisfaction or lack of it are the most reliable predictors of joy or suffering and of the stability of life itself. As Damasio puts it, human survival

> depends on the equilibrium of life functions and consequently on life regulation.... [T]he status of life regulation is expressed in the form of affects—joy, sorrow—and is modulated by appetites.[33]

These five desires are ultimate in two senses. They promote the biological survival of the individual (through foresight and the pursuit of well-being), and of groups (through fostering cooperation). Cooperation is a key to both survival and reproductive fitness. The five are also ethically ultimate in that their satisfaction (or lack of it) is among the most reliable predictors of joy or suffering. Evolutionary psychology studies the mechanisms, including motives, that cause individuals to join groups for cooperation. In turn, in my case, a form of utilitarianism, is concerned with the ethical implications of these findings.

Collectively, the intuitions that favor honoring these five ultimate desires are what I call the moral sense. Marc Hauser devotes his *Moral Minds* to affirming that such a faculty exists. He adds to it useful information derived from tests across various ethnic and class groups. These include the ability in judgments to weigh the difference between intentional and accidental consequences, and between acts and their omissions.[34] He finds that across cultures and religious faiths people make the same judgments about choices in moral dilemmas, but that their reasons are usually incoherent. Where I differ is in his claim that "our emotions are not part of the dedicated and specialized components of the moral faculty." Hauser asserts that the moral faculty processes cases in terms of causes and consequences. The verdict comes before the emotions.[35] My own studies of both Western and Chinese sources indicate the opposite. As Damasio puts it:

> ... emotion and feeling [are] not merely players in the process of reasoning, but indispensable players.... As we have argued earlier, every experience in our lives is accompanied by some degree of emotion and this is especially obvious in relation to important social and personal problems.[36]

Thus our experience of each of the five ultimate desires is in part emotional, in part cognitive, and in part motivational. In being specific about the emotions that play a role in happiness, I depart again from traditional utilitarianism. Feelings, knowing about consequences, and motives relating to instincts all may operate simultaneously.

Moral Intuitions, Choices, and Action

Our awareness of the ultimate desires is in the form of moral intuitions that influence our choices. The record of social science findings has convinced many writers that there is a certain uniformity of moral choices among humans, regardless of culture, sex, and age. One prominent biologist reports that the notion of fairness is found in "almost all aspects of human life."[37] Researchers have found that all societies share common beliefs that murder and incest are wrong (with some particular nuances), that children should be cared for, that we should be loyal to family, and that we should not lie or break promises.[38] Another biologist says that we all inherit regularities of development in anatomy, cognition, and conduct.[39] Others say that many of our choices derive from sympathy and the evolutionary benefits of cooperation.[40] These choices result from moral intuitions that have survival value. As one biologist puts it, "We have cognitive processes that allow us to make quick moral decisions that will increase the likelihood of survival."[41] Another writes, "Most of the time our inclination toward fair play or our sympathy for the plight of others are immediate and instinctive, a reflex of our emotions more than an act of our intellect...."[42] Their findings suggest that a knowledge of the inborn patterns of social choice can help us understand the evolutionary factors linked to some moral choices.

Over time, lots of terms have been used in China and in the West to refer to what I will call intuitions. In China, some have spoken of innate knowledge (*liangzhi, liangxin*). Where I would have used the word intuitions, one Western philosopher used the term "attitude," and held that, as attitudes, these basic sources of choice differ among cultures. For example, some cultures stress honor/shame more than others.[43] I would treat the quest for honor and the avoidance of shame in variable forms as universal intuitions that transcend cultural differences. Others give their own specific definitions of intuitions, such as unconscious learning gained while studying some other topic.[44]

In my own case, moving beyond the distinction between instincts and intuitions made in the previous section, I will treat moral intuitions from the perspective of evolutionary psychology. That is to say, moral intuitions are shaped by a mix of cognitive, emotional, and motivational outputs of the neural circuits in the brain.

The *cognitive* part involves beliefs, that is, interpretations about what an event is, and about whether it is right or wrong, good or bad. The emotional part taps into memories and also motivates us to act. Individually, the intuitions emerge after humans react instinctively to a stimulus. One cognitive neuroscientist says:

> ... our species instinctively reacts to events, and in a specialized system of the human brain that reaction is interpreted. Out of that interpretation, beliefs emerge about rules to live by. Sometimes they have a moral character; sometimes they are of an utterly practical nature.[45]

Treated together, the moral intuition structure constitutes what has been called the *moral sense.*

The *belief systems* that humans embrace often concern prudential rules of conduct—what we regard as necessary to achieve a sense of well-being. Some of these beliefs satisfy our ultimate desires more efficiently than others do. Others are based on our understanding of the likely consequences to the choices we make. Some of the experiences that shape our beliefs and feelings are interpreted by the brain via mirror neurons. These neurons provide both cognitive and empathic clues to the brain, based on the individual's own direct experience and his or her sympathetic reaction to the experiences of others.[46] In forming our beliefs, we make use of concepts, language, and images, all of which involve systems in the brain that do not in themselves have anything to do with morality. As Damasio puts it:

> Moreover, the systems that support ethical behavior are probably not dedicated to ethics exclusively. They are dedicated to biological regulation, memory, decision-making, and creativity.[47]

Emotions or *feelings* attach themselves to memories or beliefs that are used in reasoning and emerge as intuitions. These in turn trigger our interpretations about rules, empathic experiences, and means to satisfy a desire. Damasio also says:

> [The] emotional signal can operate entirely under the radar of consciousness. It can produce alterations in working memory, attention, and reasoning so that the decision-making process is biased toward selecting the action most likely to lead to the best possible outcome, given prior experience.... In these conditions we intuit a decision and enact it, speedily and efficiently, without any knowledge of the intermediate steps.[48]

Pinker puts it this way: "People have gut feelings that give them emphatic moral convictions.... They arise from the neurobiological and evolutionary design of the organs we call moral emotions."[49] The moral emotions include anger and disgust (useful for punishing cheaters), gratitude (toward altruists), sympathy, compassion, and pride/shame.

So a gut feeling can suggest that a person does not make the kind of choice that in the past had negative emotional consequences. Thereby it increases the efficiency of reasoning.

The mirror neurons are central to our ability to intuit the feelings and experiences of others and then form beliefs about them. This is the root of the sympathy—and the altruism—found at the core of many ethical systems.

Now to the *motives* that form part of intuitions. As Michael Gazzaniga puts it, our emotions provide the impetus for the actions we decide to take:

> [W]hen someone is willing to *act* on a moral belief, it is because the emotional part of his or her brain has become active when considering the moral question at hand.[50]

Once an action is selected, the individual or others can decide if the choice is or is not a good one. For example, a person sometimes might consider whether a choice is consistent with the rule of reciprocity. The early Confucians understood that the moral mind is also an evaluative organ. The *shifei zhi xin* (mind of right and wrong) not only comprehends (cognition, beliefs) right and wrong, but also approves (*shi*) the one and disapproves (*fei*) the other. The latter are emotions leading to a motive to act.

The moral sense must compete with other desires, such as for wealth, power, or sex. We, as moral beings, must reject the common mistake of saying that the existence of biological roots in a desire bestows legitimacy on it. Steven Pinker illustrates this in his response to some commentators on the book, *The Natural History of Rape* (2000).[51] Pinker rejects the notion that the existence of gang rape among primates justifies sexual coercion by human males. As he argues, the error in this interpretation is that biology does not tell us what is moral or immoral. It reveals patterns or tendencies. For me, this means it may be useful to men to know about tendencies for which they need to be alert so as to control them. But awareness of the biological sources of sexual desire cannot ethically trump awareness of the *ultimate desire* for autonomy felt by women, as by all humans. That includes autonomy or control over their own bodies. Here is a classic case of conflict between competing desires in which the moral sense, involving one of the ultimate desires, identifies which desire should win.

The moral sense itself is usually an efficient and positive guide, when not dominated by ideology or negative emotions. It is secured by our commitments to the values identified by the intuitions. But not all gut feelings and subsequent choices are valid. Some choices are hampered by incomplete information about likely consequences. The missing information may be about practical matters, or it may show that the choice is inconsistent with the fulfillment of one of the other ultimate desires. Or, an individual's moral intuition may fail to conform to society's ethical standard. For me, any attempt to coerce my choice such that it requires me to care as much for people I will never know, as I do for those with whom I am close, violates the two-realm standard. In addition, such a choice would be impractical, because I have minimal ability to help those I do not know. However, as the internet, mass media, and foreign travel bring disparate members of the world into closer contact, our sense of altruism toward "the other" expands.

Mirror Neurons

The mirror neurons are a promising link between biology and culture. Although much remains to be learned and confirmed about them, they seem basic to how the individual learns skills, including language. They permit the individual to observe how a teacher is acting, and then transform those images into motor acts. At the same time, mirror neurons may facilitate the transmission of culture from one generation to the next. Each new generation learns from the previous one by observing and imitating their actions in contexts important to the well-being of the society.

The mirror neurons also reveal one of the most effective ways to learn to act on intuitions: by simulation. Simulation involves imitating the experience of other people in a certain situation. It also involves imagining how we would experience a situation, from what we know about ourselves and also from what we know of others, whom we mentally imitate. In many fields, learning through simulation involves using a model, such as operating a flight simulator, practicing medical diagnostics with an artificial model of a patient, or negotiating with role-playing students who "represent" business rivals. Among other things, the learner tries to imitate what she expects the instructor or other parties to do and experience, and how they would evaluate her.

We can practice what we have learned through simulation when the bright light of moral intuition flashes in our minds. Through experience and imagination we can anticipate how things will turn out for us if we act on an intuition. Recent studies reveal that learning through simulations increases skill level to a greater degree than does any book-based training.

Public Morality

My own ultimate desires become part of public morality when I understand that other people have them as well, beginning with my own family, neighbors, and outsiders with whom I have bonded in some activity or organization. My interest extends to the presence of the desires in all people, but this is where predictable political and legal protections should play the central protective and nurturing role. The United Nations Universal Declaration of Human Rights identifies some of these essential desires.

I strongly support such legal bodies as the United Nations and its agencies. Public morality involves recognizing that helping others fulfill their desires is a way of fulfilling them myself.[52] The support comes from having a commitment to and respect for the law when it is properly legislated. It also involves charity toward those organizations that also contribute to the protection and nurturance of the rights of others, motivated by whatever sympathy the individual experiences.

I also believe we must share information about how to fulfill those ultimate desires. This includes technology and knowledge about public natural resources, such as air, water, and trees. Sharing information is an important aspect of reciprocal altruism, and such cooperation benefits everyone. I will highlight the importance of sharing information in the Part Two, on moral choices in choices about global warming.

Social Emotions, Conformity, and Independence

When a moral intuition suddenly appears, illuminating an action choice, how does a person go from insight to doing something about it? In traditional Chinese ethics, the question would be, "How do we combine knowing and doing?" In my study, I would ask how a choice would help fulfill one or more of the five ultimate desires. Recall Gazzaniga's words that

> ... [W]hen someone is willing to *act* on a moral belief, it is because the emotional part of his or her brain has become active when considering the moral question at hand.[53]

Emotions such as contentment and tranquility help repair or rejuvenate the body. Other emotions protect it. Fear spurs us to escape from harm, anger to attack an enemy, shame to withdraw. Sometimes we use one emotion to counter another, as when we feel empathy for a culprit, thus assuaging our anger. So emotions are often adaptive, promoting the individual's well-being. Shame/honor or respect can encourage cooperation in a group. But culture informs how these feelings are expressed and interpreted. Richard Brandt noticed the variations in how honor is expressed in the cultures of southern and northern United States.[54] Among the emotions significant in ethics, guilt, shame/respect, and trust stand out.

Guilt and Shame/Respect

Shame is a panhuman or universal social emotion, though culture determines the conditions under which it arises.[55] According to Daniel Fessler's studies in Sumatra, most (87%) of the expressions of shame (*malu*) follow a six-point logic. Its core is the individual's violating a rule, being aware of the violation, and being aware that others know of the violation. In the remainder of cases, the emotion can arise when the individual is in the presence of a superior.

In China, shame (*xiuchi, xiukui*) and pride (*zizunxin*) come as a punishment-reward set. In classical Chinese, honor (*rong*) is the external source of pride, bestowed in the form of titles, banners, monumental stone markers, and special privileges. A sense of inner worth is the other source. The *Liji* (Book of Rites) makes the point that even in a famine, a self-respecting person refuses food when it is offered with a rude shout of, "Hey! Come here and eat!" (*jielai zhi shi*).[56] Such a person has an inner moral compass. For purposes of this study, I will focus mainly on shame. The three components that comprise shame (feeling, cognition, and motivation) also apply to honor/pride, with their contents reversed.

The official public use of shame and honor has been inherited regularly up to the present. I refer to the use of negative and positive models. An extreme example of the use of negative models is the public execution of certain criminals, not simply as punishment but also as a lesson. As for positive models, they are always in vogue. The Chinese Ministry of Education recently debated whether or not they should revise an elementary school text to change the existing models, the "five great heroes of the War against Japan." The suggestion from Shanghai was to replace them with a contemporary figure, Liu Xiang, China's first Olympic gold medalist in the track and field event (110 meter hurdle), a good model of the competitive spirit. The Ministry opted to keep the old models, perhaps mindful that competitive profit-seeking by sport stars may not be an enduring value. Recently Nanjing East Road Neighborhood Committee in Shanghai introduced a program of public shaming of persons who were unfilial, or inadequately caring of their aged parents. In April 2006, China's leaders started a national campaign named "Eight Honors and Disgraces." They also supported the public shaming of the Chinese computer scientist, Chen Jin, accused of fraudulent claims.[57]

This management technique has been used successfully by a broad range of practitioners, from photographers and cartoonists to essayists and public speakers. Through picture and words, they effectively shape behavior by appealing to the public's potent fear of shame (or desire for honor).

Shame is not embarrassment, and it is not guilt, though speakers may casually use shame and embarrassment interchangeably. It concerns diminished self-worth, based in part on knowledge that others know that one has broken a rule. One prominent study of the emotions in China says, "For the most part, scholars identify the concept of shame with that of 'face'."[58] I disagree. In discussing shame, I am not talking about "face" (*mianzi* in traditional terminology, or *lian* in contemporary speech), as in "loss of face." "Face" concerns some challenge to my fixed social position. For example, if my wife were to criticize me in front of my office colleagues, this might cause me *embarrassment* (loss of face), but not shame. In embarrassment there is no attack, by others or by myself, on my moral worth. There is with shame.

Nor am I talking about "guilt." Shame is not guilt in the sense of culpability for a crime (*zui, zui'e gan*). Nor is it guilt in the sense of a sin (also *zui*). There are plenty of references to that kind of guilt in the morality books (*shanshu*, lit. good books) in traditional China, with their tales of retribution for sins committed against gods or spirits. As Daniel Fessler has said, a person can experience guilt about an act, such as adultery, even if no one else knows anything about it. Only the actor knows (along with, perhaps, God). In contrast, other people's knowledge of the transgression is crucial to shame. No transcendental deities need be involved in one's feelings of shame. Rather, shame relates to one's sense of moral worth within society.

As Kwong-loi Shun noted, one of the best English translations of the early terms that we now know as shame is disdain.[59] The two terms differ, of course, in significant ways. Disdain refers to the contemptuous attitude of an outside evaluator, whereas shame describes one's internal sense of humiliation and loss of status. In the *Analects*, the term for shame is *chi*.[60] It focuses on publicly visible facts about the self, such as character defects that prevent one from following the Way. Consciousness of these flaws and a disdain for them constitute a person's control mechanism that encourages conformity and protects him from physical punishment from external enforcers. This inner mechanism helps him to identify personal qualities that are morally inferior and might lower his self-worth, and it moves him to avoid or change those perceived defects. Already in the *Analects* we find that shame (an emotion) is related to a knowledge (cognition) of the rules of propriety; with such knowledge, the person's conduct will manifest conformance that all can see:

> If the people be led by laws, and uniformity sought to be given them by punishments, they will try to avoid the punishment, but have no sense of shame. If they be led by virtue [virtuous models], and uniformity sought to be given them by rules of propriety, they will have a sense of shame, and moreover will become good.[61]

On guilt, there is no scholarly consensus. For some thinkers, guilt is a result of a breach of responsibility;[62] for others, a lack of positive motivation. Gibbard says it is a response to the expectation of anger from others. Fessler says it is not affected by the opinion of others.[63] A popular position is that guilt is less prominent in China than in the West because in China, individual identity is conceived in relational terms. That is, an individual is wife, mother, daughter, of X village, in Y province, attached to Z work place.[64] The individual tends to act responsibly in circumscribed ways. In my opinion both guilt and shame help motivate an individual to act in ways that avoid conflict and negative sanctions from others. Where guilt is not the direct result of negative opinions of others, it may involve a perception of acting against God's rules, as in "guilt before God." In this situation, an act of infidelity may cause guilt even though no other person knows about it. On the other hand, shame is always a response to the possible disdain of others.[65] In China shame is linked to morality when it is used to enforce fulfillment of social duties arising from the aforementioned relational obligations.

Shame/respect promote conformity and cooperation. The individual violates a rule, in positive law, custom, or a professional rule of conduct. He is aware of the breach, and knows that others know of it, too. The others express disdain for the breach. Empathy helps the individual read signals from others. It enables one to predict how others are likely to act toward her.[66] Such predictions concern consequences of choices open to her to continue or discontinue a deviant act. By such foresight and planning, one can make choices that promote cooperation.

When one foresees the goals of others and what might be their reaction to the individual's own acts, she may benefit the group. Shame/respect are among the chief means of a group's social control, and they have a biological basis. When the neurotransmitter serotonin emerged in human evolution, it adapted to social hierarchy. Respect raises it; shame lowers it. A person's inclusion in cooperative activity, along with group benefits, depends on her meeting the expectations of others or conforming to their rules.

Such rules, for example, might express fairness or equal sharing.[67] Those rules might also govern how and when emotions are expressed. They may be moral codes. Among other things, morality involves compliance with or violation of rules or guidelines set down by a group or society. This includes political agents who use public praise or shame as tools for enforcing conformance with rules. These tools may be embedded in laws, dictated by the state. China's history of local and central governments establishing positive and negative models used respect and shame as control devices. Shame can be experienced by groups and is often called humiliation. It is a powerful tool in political movements. For example, many historians say that some restrictions placed on Germany after World War I at Versailles had as their aim humiliating the Germans. Political events reactive to the humiliation followed. Some suicide bombers have revealed effects of humiliation brought on by foreign occupation.

Trust

According to some evolutionary thought, people seek consistency because it is associated with conformity to group rules, which in turn enhances cooperation. Cooperation fosters individual and group evolutionary survival and reproductive success. The proximate or immediate reason people seek predictability is that it reduces stress, as measured in part by levels of cortisol. When the individual feels in control of situations, it benefits her health and is pleasurable. Trust and consistency go together. And because natural selection works at the individual and group level, so do both shame/respect and trust.

In its modern usage in the West, trust has recently been defined this way. It is "a psychological state comprising the intention to accept vulnerability based upon positive expectations of the intentions or behavior of another."[68] The vulnerability exists because the trusted party may try to get some selfish advantage from the trustor without giving any reciprocity or benefit. Trust comes when for some reason, that trustor accepts, ignores, or overrides her vulnerability. For example, she believes in the integrity of the other. Or they may have a long relationship. This integrity can be enhanced by adding transparency and shared information, which may benefit a prospective trustee.

For our understanding of the Chinese roots of the idea of trust, we have the work of Professor An Yanming, *The Idea of* Cheng *(Sincerity/Reality): Its Formation in the History of Chinese Philosophy.*[69] He finds that a precursor of the philosophical term *cheng* was *xin* (trust). It referred to a quality of words and deeds that elicited trust from others. The term *shi* referred to reality or truth. These early notions later emerged in the two core meanings of *cheng*.

The first meaning answers the question, "How can a person gain trust from others?" The answer is where there is consistency or correspondence, between that person's words and his deeds. The second meaning has to do with the essential attribute of a thing, and when it applies to the self, means "to be true to oneself" or to have integrity. This may involve having integrated or complimentary traits or motives.

In these Confucian texts, *cheng* will often mean the trait to which self-cultivation leads, namely spontaneous consistency between words and deeds, while mindful of the inner standards or moral sense one holds. There can be no self-deception. The person watches over himself even when alone (the term is *shendu*, used in the text *Daxue*, the Great Learning). The cognitive part includes awareness of the words-deeds correspondence and of the essential moral sense that should guide them, making the person authentic or real. As a philosophical term, *cheng* appears in the *Mencius* describing a desire to please one's parents. There are both a feeling component and a cognitive understanding of what is good.[70]

So the An study concludes that consistency has a core place in the early Chinese use of the term *cheng*. It is also a basic Confucian value. Today *chengxin* constitutes a compound, meaning trustworthiness. It is a behavioral trait by which other people regard someone as deserving of trust. And *chengshi* is a character trait whose high status deserves to be restored in today's society.

Trust is a societal value that takes root in individual relationships. As a societal value, it is essential for the stability of a non-coercive relation between leaders and led, whether in a small group or in a state. It emerges when one or more persons expect others to honor an exchange of benefits (honor the trust). This involves *fairness in reciprocity*, where culture decides on the rules that determine what are *equal* or *reciprocal* benefits.[71] Those benefits do not need to be the same in quantity. Vulnerability exists when one party (the one being trusted, or trustee) has an opportunity to exploit the trustor for personal gain. The two parties have different interests, trustors caring more about risk and trustees more about the level of benefit they may receive.[72]

Deepak Malhotra has studied the trust situations in which the incentive to exploit has been trumped by the trustor's deterrence power or ability to punish, by the character reputation of the trustee, or by the kind of relationship between the parties. For example, in a long-term relationship, people stop calculating the risks/benefits of the trust relation.

Just as shame/respect promote cooperative behavior, so does trust. It facilitates prediction of what another person will do. This is achieved through empathy and by reading trust signals that indicate that a person is trustworthy. Signals might include anything, from forms of greeting, to making a point of doing what one had promised to do. Information sharing also helps. The cooperative behavior is reinforced in part because trust is pleasurable. Interestingly, such pleasure outcomes have been studied by measuring the oxytocin and dopamine levels of the trusting parties.[73]

Trusting relationships are enhanced by something beyond promoting conformance to ethical rules. Enhanced by commitment, this bond may reduce the need for keeping track of mutual benefits.[74]

Independence

Whereas I recognize the positive role of shame/respect and trust in supporting conformity with rules and cooperation that fulfill mutual desires, this does not mean that I prize conformity to the point of ignoring autonomy of choice. In my mind they coexist. There are the moral intuitions that promote cooperation, such as sympathy and altruism, and fairness/reciprocity. We ourselves are the sources of such values as equality and fairness, though our cultures contribute. There are also intuitions that lead to the wish for independent choice. The ability to control such choices enhances the ability to choose good outcomes, also allowing for creative responses. There is pleasure in mastery and in risk taking.

Groups also benefit from foresight wherein members share information about future outcomes. Often such predictions vary, as individuals compete within the group for success. Examples abound in the natural sciences. Science has always been something of a social enterprise. Diversity of beliefs fosters the discovery of new ideas. This is especially true today. As we look at the authors of journal papers, we find that there may be five or twenty of them. Each may independently contribute her own stance at parts of the discovery process, exhibiting her independent judgments. Others may contest some of the judgments, to the extent of leading to conformity in the final positions and resultant public product. Peer review brings the social process back into this complex mix of independence and group pressure.

Foresight and the Politics of Free Choice

In recent years, some people have rejected the belief that there is a human nature. One reason is their assumption that identifying fairly universal forms of social behavior and emotions is the same as determinism, namely that our personal choices do not count and we cannot control what we do. This ignores the fact that behavior is a combined product of genes and the environment, including culture, and varies accordingly. Also, just because nature predisposes us to act in certain ways, such as by making it pleasant to do so, does not mean we cannot choose otherwise. As some have pointed out,[75] I can ignore my sex drive and have fewer children than I am capable of, or become a monk. Persons may reject the idea of human nature because they see a danger that some advocates of it will claim that whatever is "natural" is good or right and use this faulty reasoning to legitimize what others would perceive as their own evil acts. But reasoning from natural to good or evil is faulty. Most of those in the new evolutionary sciences believe that there is nothing morally praiseworthy or the opposite about products of evolution. As Steven Pinker has written, many praiseworthy acts are unnatural, such as being faithful to a spouse, or believing that all children have equal value.[76] Praiseworthy acts often require moral choices, combining what we know as facts about human nature, with a value standard.[77] The facts about human nature are the instincts that evolve into the five moral intuitions and thereby contribute to joy or suffering. Second, I should examine the actual alternative scenarios. Then I should choose the one that most effectively coincides with values in my standard: bodily well-being, love (sympathy, empathy, altruism, as the case may be), fairness (expressed in reciprocity, trust), respect, and foresight plus control of a resulting choice.

To reassure those who fear that biology is tied to determinism, they can be mindful that making choices is something our brains are designed by nature to do. Choices often follow from learning something, another innate instinct, part of the brain's architecture. We are able to change beliefs and make new choices as a result of what we have learned. Sometimes an event in the environment affects our development by switching genes on and off. As Matt Ridley puts it:

> Experiments confirm the complexity, plasticity, and circularity of the system but also reveal that even the environment affects development only [*sic.*] by switching genes on and off—genes that allow plasticity and learning.[78]

Learning

At a cellular level learning involves strengthening synapses. Genes design the neurons, and each one has about seventy synapses connecting it to other neurons. The brain requires dopamine neurons or cells to react to bad predictions with surprise and flag positive outcomes. This is where learning occurs, in the process behind making and revising choices.[79] So some choice making is a joint product of environment, plus genes and development stages. Other human traits are more strongly inherited, such as I.Q. and personality, though even then experience and culture play a role.

Politics and Free Choice

The topic of free choice becomes a political issue when, for reasons of politics, power, or money, people claim that there is no enduring human nature. They want to justify social engineering, to control choices to fit their own political agendas. This means ignoring the individual's control over her choices, thus ignoring the basic moral intuitions or ultimate desires, rooted in instincts, that are relevant to ethical choices.

The behaviorist B. F. Skinner advocated social engineering. Before him, Lenin claimed that human nature can be trained or molded into a "new man," who would be part of his communist system. Obviously, this gave power to Lenin, Mao, and other modern leaders who claim to act as guides or teachers, aiming to transform our minds.[80] In recent decades in the United States, many anthropologists follow in the Leninist path claiming that the principal agent of human nature is culture, not biology.

Contrary to the belief of some social engineers, free choice exists. It does have limits, but less the manipulative products of the engineers than instincts and desires that resist their conditioning. A famous experiment by Harry Harlow in 1958 proved that the mother-infant bond trumps attempts to replace it with Skinner's transitory rewards.[81] That was a watershed in the declining influence among psychologists of Skinner's behaviorist psychology. There are predispositions or behavioral tendencies that both limit the success of the engineers on the one hand and contextualize free choices on the other hand. A choice is free when it is the product not of coercion but of my decision, even though that decision is influenced by my natural or social environment.

To accept natural limits on free choice, as many scientists do, has been attacked as "racism," that to accept such limits is to accept the social status quo of racial and class inequalities. It is to discourage people from trying to change the status quo. Critics of evolutionary psychology or socio-biology want no limits on the individual's menu of possible choices.[82]

Ultimate Desires and the Two-Realm Standard

Humans possess biological predispositions to forms of social behavior, or tendencies over which genes have a statistical influence. But other influences can modify or reject the choices to which they lead. This is one place for moral commitments to step in and motivate behavior. Choices I make on the basis of a moral system can be free. For example, we have innate tendencies to be greedy, to seek power, and to inflict harm on others. But we have competing predispositions. As discussed before, one is for foresight about the consequences of our actions and those of other people, and our wish for control over the consequences. Another is for empathy toward others. These competing tendencies are consistent with the value of cooperation and can be activated against the negative tendencies. We are genetically receptive to cooperative behavior. The emotions of sympathy and trust lead us to seek cooperators. Our innate facility with language helps us to share technical information that promotes group well-being and fitness. So human nature is a mixture of the instinct-based moral intuitions that foster cooperation, and the darker urges to pursue greed and aggression.

The prefrontal cortex is the locus of the brain that functions to inhibit behavior by anticipating predictable consequences according to our two-realm standard. The content of that standard is joy and pain avoidance, measured by fulfilling the five ultimate desires: *health and well-being of the body, love (including the desire to be loved) and sympathy, fairness (bound up with trust and reciprocity), respect (manifest in prizing esteem and avoiding shame),* and *foresight (plus control over our choices).* Within the family or community this part of the brain can help us make choices in how we use our resources—monetary and emotional—to foster well-being. Within the framework of the larger public, those same brain functions help us to predict how the law or other citizens will respond to our choices. This may include the expectation of punishment. Sometimes punishment is built into the law as a deterrent to socially harmful behavior, and works best when it is predictable or certain. Positively, the law can help secure for the public the protections and nurturance that promote the joy and avoidance of sorrow.

Our major assets in trying to do the right thing belong to both nature and nurture (the environment, experience, culture). To nature we owe our ability to have empathy and foresight (getting into the minds of others). This is why the 1991 discovery of the mirror neurons by Rizzolatti is so important. But nurture enters too, in the modes by which we accumulate, share, and transmit knowledge. We begin by using our innate ability to anticipate the behavior of other people and to imitate them and communicate. Then we use cultural forms to gather and transfer what we learn. In this way we can use the wisdom of others, sometimes the elders, about the consequences of various choices and when to be creative in them. Cultures can change one another through give and take of technologies. Such was the case with those in China who learned of stirrups and saddles from the Mongols.

Conclusion

In Part Two, I will apply the ethical guidelines developed in Part One to two public issues. Both affect China and also have wider implications: moral choices about global warming, and the lack of consistency in the judicial system. Though focusing on public issues, I will make references to the private sphere. My standard will be the two-realm utilitarianism and the five ultimate desires by which that standard can be realized.

I will show that the five ultimate desires suggest some specific choices. In the first example, global warming, I will establish the roles of *reciprocity* in the sharing of technical information, *foresight* about the consequences of alternative choices in the *health* of future generations, and *respect or esteem, and shame* as group sanctions to support our choices. Those sanctions will also appear with greater attention in the second example, concerning the Chinese judicial system. *Sympathy* plays a part in both examples, influencing how individuals act on shared knowledge to make choices that affect the well-being of their present and future kin and on their communities. *Consistency* that often facilitates *foresight* is a key value that can support a legal system by fostering trust between leaders and led. *Learning by imitation* (simulation, model emulation) will appear as a useful training device for practicing choice-making that reflects the five desires.

Most of the ultimate desires are interrelated. Several link together as a cluster. At their core is usually the *equal worth* of all humans, based on their shared traits. This includes their common quest for healthy survival, experienced as joy and the absence of suffering. At the same time, equality is linked to *fairness*, in that access to clean air and water and health care should be shared by all. Equality is related to *reciprocity* in that part of the meaning of fairness is equal sharing. Acting with fairness involves cooperation, in order to generate the conditions for common clean air and water and general health care. Finally, in both the public and private sectors, equality of worth is related to *trust*. Only with fairness does trust emerge. Trust is essential for non-coercive relations in the public and private spheres.

A different cluster includes foresight, trust, and autonomy. Having foresight of the consequences of policies and of individual choices promotes cooperation. Foresight is normally facilitated by trust. In the Chinese case, this involves consistency or predictability in matters such as words and deeds, with exceptions (wartime deception). In the case of individuals, autonomy can be prized because it provides control over the choices a person makes, based on foresight of likely consequences of the actions of the individual or of others. This cluster may lead people to say that they can foresee the consequences of global warming for children and grandchildren, and choose to support policies at home and nationally that try to reduce the impact of those consequences.

Finally, the desire for respect or esteem in family or community and in larger groups is a source of motivation. Clustered with its opposite, shame, the two are innate social emotions that suggest powerful tools which can be useful in realizing the other ultimate desires for all people and for family.

2

Application One: Bad Hurricanes and Rising Sea Levels

Moral Complexities in Choices about Global Warming

For many people in Asia, global warming seems to be such a gigantic topic that they push it out of their minds, as something too vague and huge to warrant attention. Continued economic growth is their main concern. I reply with a bit of optimism that there are plenty of things we can do to lessen the impact of long term global warming, and there is precedent for success. In the United States, strong laws were passed in the 1970s to control smog. Since then, air pollution has dropped by a third to a half. Acid rain has dropped by a third since the 1990 Clean Air Act requiring sulfur-dioxide emission reductions, and two technical innovations (the catalytic converter and a chemical process to remove certain pollutants from gasoline).[1]

Now, with this newly understood danger of climate change, the technology does exist to make life conducive to our well-being and to that of our offspring. But politically we are at an impasse as to how to get there. I want to suggest how to judge alternative proposals for getting around that political impasse, involving China and the United States.

My method begins with identifying the human values that are most relevant to the issue of climate change, especially global warming. To argue for any policies in terms of core ethical values is more powerful than appealing only to the economic model of material or monetary cost-benefit. In the United States, those who say that only economic benefits count assume that people are interested *only* in maximizing their own profit. The new science of evolutionary psychology has shown that this is a false picture of human motivation. It is too simple. People are also innately motivated by devotion to and responsibility for family and community, by sympathy, by avoidance of shame and the quest for respect, and by an interest in trust. So the model that says people are motivated only by self-interest and greed is psychologically false. It is also morally incomplete.

Two ethical values are relevant to climate change. One is the equal worth of all humans. In the United States this principle is contained in the phrase, "All men are created equal" in the Declaration of Independence; it is also reflected in the Mayflower Compact of 1620 which referred to "just and equal laws," and in the Fourteenth Amendment to the Constitution (1868) requiring equal treatment under the law. In China, a similar value imbues the Mencian pronouncement: "The sage and I are the same in kind."[2] In the United Nations Universal Declaration of Human Rights, the wording is that all people are "equal in dignity and rights." Today this value should be manifest in equal treatment under domestic and international law, especially in matters of health and education. Equal treatment is the operational form of equal worth; otherwise, equality is only a contemplative vision. The second value relevant to climate change is reciprocity, the basis of cooperation, on which biological survival often depends.

I hold that these are universal values. A belief in equal worth presumes that all people, including future generations, deserve to lead healthy lives. This is one reason that I believe that the central governments of the United States and China must intervene to honor serious environmental goals. Our awareness of the consequences of global warming indicates the kind of policies we should support at the national and international levels to slow down its path. Likewise, families and communities in the private sphere must make environmentally responsible choices, with their own children and grandchildren in mind.

Provinces, states, and cities each play a role as well—but in the long term disparate local initiatives, crucial at first, are not likely to be as efficient as centrally mandated guidance and solutions. Different cities often have different standards, which, among other things, is not good for business planning.

My slogan is "*clean* and renewable energy." I strongly support the continued use of known renewable energy sources, such as windmills, solar power, and biofuels. But alone, these renewables are insufficient to solve the global warming problem. I will focus on an example of a new "clean energy" technology called Carbon Capture and Storage (CCS). One form is "ultra-supercritical pulverized coal" (USC). Another, Integrated Gasification Combined Cycle (IGCC), involves capturing the carbon dioxide from coal as it is burned to generate electricity. For short, it is called "coal gasification." Both involve storing the captured carbon in underground geological formations. Another related opportunity is updating China's industrial boilers, used in light industry, textile mills, and heating for apartment blocks. These boilers consume 40% of Chinese coal.[3]

In the United States, some utility CEOs agree about the need to build gasification plants. This is true of NRG Energy, which is planning a plant in Tonawanda, New York, and of American Electric Power, whose spokesman said that there is demonstrable evidence that separating carbon from gasified coal is superior to doing so at a pulverized coal plant. They plan to build two gasification plants. No one denies there is still engineering work ahead, and gasification has its skeptics. On the basis of my own research, however, I favor proceeding with gasification technology. Even if, in a worst case, it does not fulfill expectations, my main point in using it as an example still holds: to stress the value and possibility of reciprocity, including technology sharing, in our dealing with China on global warming matters.

People who are serious about slowing global warming should make the moral arguments for going the road of the new coal technology. This technology is little known except by energy specialists. A broad coalition of experts, environmentalists, and policy-makers must argue loudly and clearly on behalf of this "cleaner" energy. Indeed, when General Electric started its clean coal program in 2005, its Chairman and CEO said that he was initiating the program, "not because it is trendy or moral, but because it will accelerate [economic growth]."[4] That is exactly the style of half-way justifications that I wish to reject as incomplete. The moral justification, based as it is on the consequence of global warming for the healthy lives of all people today and the health of future generations, gives the strongest additional support that advocacy can find. The moral argument can then be paired with a new economic argument about the benefits of innovation in new technologies that produce energy that is clean and renewable. Companies facing new laws or edicts curbing emissions must and will innovate. Fortunately, a coalition of experts did speak in Paris on February 2, 2007. This was the Intergovernmental Panel on Climate Change, that reports to the United Nations. Their finding is that warming is most likely caused by carbon dioxide and other heat trapping gases. As the emissions are due to human actions, the warming will continue unless those gases are curbed.

Here is the current situation. Fossil fuels provide 80% of the world's energy. Energy use is rapidly rising. It drives economic growth, which most people prize. Nuclear power cannot provide enough electricity. Other electric energy sources may be developed in the future. But coal is the single energy source that the United States and China, the two biggest energy users, have in abundance (enough for roughly another 160 years). However, coal-burning emissions negatively affect human health, and the carbon dioxide in them is already causing global warming. In China, sulfur dioxide contributes each year to nearly 400,000 early deaths. We need to act because the problems of global warming are with us now. If we are going to act, we need ethically informed guidelines.

At present, China has three problems that impede some choices. First, in its competitive economy, industries are often unresponsive to government direction. There are different zones of decision making or fragmentation when it comes to regulating the industries that create or could restrain emissions and pollutants. Plants often ignore the government rulings. Local officials routinely do not enforce laws to lessen air and water pollution. Individual plants often ignore central government rules about filtering systems, going so far as to buy them but refusing to use them because of electricity costs. In spite of a 2005 central government policy to reduce emissions by 20% by 2010, economic growth remains for most local officials the top priority, higher than lowering emissions.

The second problem derives from the rapid increase of demand for electricity and resulting fear of power shortages. No central government agency encourages existing local utility plants to get rid of outdated, inefficient equipment. Rushing to answer the demand for power, local areas often choose small-scale generating plants using old technology. Low energy prices obstruct raising the capital for introducing the new clean coal or more efficient machinery that can reduce emissions. The local Chinese governments place the ancient value of "social stability" ahead of reducing emissions and pollution, not wanting to anger customers and foster inflation by raising prices.[5]

The third problem is that China wants foreign companies to transfer technology secrets, which the companies do not wish to do. Technology transfer works best when there is also manufacturing transfer of relevant equipment. In the absence of such exchanges, the Chinese are likely to receive many educational demonstrations but little dissemination of the new techniques.[6]

Neither the United States nor China has an operational energy policy. They both need one that stresses renewable energy sources, the efficient use and reduced consumption of oil, the construction of new electric generating plants that use clean coal, and upgraded industrial boilers for industrial and apartment buildings. China has had success in setting auto emissions standards. But given erratic government regulation over existing companies, the best hope for future success lies in those areas where the central government can provide high levels of both investment and control, namely coal gasification. This is precisely where the United States is developing new technologies.

There is an international agency that facilitates technology transfer. It is the International Energy Agency (IEA). Many countries are involved, as are development banks and the Global Environmental Facility (GEF).[7] The main information provider, formed in 1975, is the IEA's Clean Coal Center, and also the World Coal Institute, a global non-profit NGO.

With an agreement to cooperate and share information and equipment, China and the United States could make a change in the trajectory of global warming. Agreements at the government level are needed to move forward on this urgent task. They would require China to stop subsidizing cheap electricity and use capital from higher customer charges to build new plants. China would ask the United States for technology transfer; in exchange China would agree to buy new equipment and plants designed by American companies like General Electric. Eventually, the two countries would be sharing their new technology. Bilateral or trilateral governmental policies would help realize the ethical values that I will now identify more fully.

Values: Equal Worth, and Reciprocity

Distributional equality is not the same thing as equal human worth. It refers instead to a utopian way of dividing the world's resources. Attempts to implement equal divisions of resources have always ended in disaster, in terms of economic loss and human suffering. Go back in China's history and recall the failure of the well-field system (*jingtian*) in the Song dyansty, and the damage Maoist egalitarian policies caused in modern China. In contrast, the principle of *equal worth* has a strong record of success, namely equal protection and treatment under the law (both nationally and internationally), and equal opportunity.

The Kyoto Protocol set good targets. Its goal was to limit global emissions of six greenhouse gases, mainly carbon dioxide. But built into the Protocol is a problem caused by its apparent assumption of the utopian idea of equal distribution of material resources.

The Kyoto Compact has a two-tiered set of mandatory obligations. In the case of industrialized countries, Kyoto requires percentage commitments by each country to reduce their greenhouse gases below 1990 levels (7% below 1990 levels for the United States), starting with its implementation in February, 2005. Developing nations such as China and India have no requirements on reductions during the period the Protocol is in effect (until 2012). Objectors say that this gives them an economic advantage over their First-World competitors. Their manufacturing costs will be less than those of G-8 competitors. American objectors include some senators of both parties and the Bush Administration. They want the same restrictions on developing nations now as would be leveled on the United States, Canada, Japan, Europe, New Zealand, and Australia.

Some Asian supporters of Kyoto have appealed to the utopian value of distributional equality in wanting no limits on their emissions. As for the principle of equality, one author quotes a former Indian prime minister as arguing that the people in the industrialized world have already had their lion's share of wealth created by emitting carbon dioxide. Why should they continue to be allowed to emit more than any other countries and continue to reap the economic benefits of utilities or companies that do so? He said, "We do not believe that the ethos of democracy can support any norm other than equal per capita rights to global environmental resources."[8] In short, this prime minister is saying there is a right to equal shares of resources. An Indian writer says:

> Equal rights to the atmosphere for all human beings and equity within and between nations are paramount. This implies for example, that reduction percentages and emissions allowances, etc., should be based on a per capita basis.[9]

But clean air and water have no agreed upon monetary value (p. 46 below). Nor do many of the other manifestations of climate change. My own reaction to this is that the idea of equal rights ("equal per capita rights") should apply not to equal shares of natural resources or emissions (distributional equality) but to protection of the health of all under a law (equality of worth). Distributional equality, in contrast, violates the pragmatic principle that says our ethical codes must be workable if we are to pay any attention to them. It is not practical to ask Americans suddenly to reduce their living standards while other people catch up on an equal per capita basis to its level. In the United States the price of oil by itself, plus a growing popular appreciation of green vehicles, are already changing forever the unjustifiable and excessive consumption of gasoline by Americans. Hopefully a new U.S. administration can develop an energy policy.

What pragmatically can work is *reciprocity*, which assumes the equal worth of all people. All humans, in other words, share an equal right to the basic natural resources needed for survival, reproduction, well-being, and freedom from pain: clean air, clean water, and an atmosphere free of toxic levels of chemicals and climate-changing greenhouse gases. This means equal protection of their health, under international law and bilateral trade treaties. It does not refer to equal shares of resources or emissions.

Reciprocity leads to cooperative benefits for all concerned, beginning with kin folk at home. This cooperation is how we have evolved as a group-based species. But reciprocity is violated if, even at the start, little is demanded of the developing countries. So the reciprocity principle requires some modification of Kyoto's two-tiered compliance criteria. To free some countries of any requirements is to suggest to people that we are not in the same boat and do not need each other's help.

The reciprocity principle does, in certain respects, put the developed countries in the position of donor. They have an ethical obligation to provide financial and technical support so that the developing countries can reduce their own emissions. But, when applied to global warming, the idea of reciprocity also opens the door to an incredible opportunity for international economic and diplomatic negotiations involving China, the United States, and India. They already share many interests leading to cooperation: reducing dependency on foreign oil, achieving stable prices, and eliminating piracy in the tanker lanes.

The impasse on global warming centers on carbon emissions from electricity-generating coal-burning power plants. China will not discuss changing its energy consumption unless the United States becomes serious about changing its consumption. The dominant American corporate view of coal burning opposes spending money on new plants unless China does so. Individual states are taking leadership roles to challenge this perspective, but they face opposition from companies that say they will not cooperate unless other U.S. states do the same. So a variety of different state rules seems to be arising. Conclusion: government leadership is crucial to breaking the impasse.

At this particular historical moment, our focus can turn to clean coal. The product of the process called IGCC is "syngas." These three steps are involved: First, powdered coal becomes a gas after mixing with water and oxygen under high heat and high pressure. Second, the gas is cooled. Sulfur, which can be sold, is removed. By burning the gas at a low temperature, which produces electricity, the nitrogen compounds can be removed. Any excess heat produces steam that runs another turbine. Finally, the carbon dioxide is captured, and, using new technology still being tested, is pumped underground.[10]

Currently, energy companies prefer to sequester the CO_2 in depleted oil reservoirs and deep coal seams. The old oil fields and seams are favored because they have been successfully used for thirty years, because they have in the past held carbon, and because the oil fields have a geological barrier that prevents the upward movement of oil (assumed to work for carbon as well). The drawback to this approach is a risk of gas leakage.

Government leadership concerns what we do with that knowledge and technology, how we agree to use it, and how we share information. Coal is still the preferred source for China and the United States for generating electricity. In the United States pressure for increasing its future use will come from the rising cost of making petroleum products, as the old oil and gas sources deplete.

However, now electricity can be generated by gasifying the coal, keeping the carbon dioxide out of the atmosphere. As for industrial boilers, the GEF started a project in 1996 to improve their thermal efficiency. If this new technology were introduced into China, raising its level to that of developed countries, China's coal consumption could be changed. The cost of clean coal technology has been declining. In the foreseeable future, it will be competitive with conventional pulverized coal used in steam plants.

Because of the various obstacles I outlined earlier, there is at present only one coal gasification IGCC plant in China, a demonstration plant, in Yantai, Shandong province. But China has begun collaborating with Australia in the field of coal gasification, through the organization The Asia-Pacific Partnership on Clean Development and Climate.[11]

What the Chinese themselves have been successfully trying is "polygeneration." This means using several different energy inputs to produce several outputs. The inputs may include biomass, coal gas, and petroleum residue. The output would be heat, electricity, and synthetic fuels.[12] For example, in the food industry, the output might be electricity, heat at various temperature levels, and compost.

The reciprocity approach endorses the goals of the Kyoto Protocol. But, along with renewable energy, this principle recognizes that power plant innovations are central to success. And a new energy policy requires something of everyone. In the case of the United States and China, reciprocity can and should be promoted in government leadership to establish a standard energy policy for all of their respective states or provinces. When this is accomplished, neither private companies nor political figures can obstruct applying the new technology by claiming that the other country or individual states or provinces are not required to make changes.

One of the agencies that oversee China's new energy policies is the China Council for International Cooperation on Environment and Development. In 2003 it recommended to the central government that it equate coal modernization with polygeneration through gasification.[13]

Other agencies involved in these plans include the Chinese Office of Global Environmental Affairs and the Ministry for Environmental Protection. In the United States, the Department of Energy is currently most interested and financially committed. It has granted US$235 million to match private funds to build an IGCC facility in Florida. Its FutureGen initiative is part of an international partnership to build the first near zero emissions power plant by 2012.[14]

In both countries, any new energy policy must include three conditions: First, establish and enforce laws regulating new cars, trucks, and power plants to slow climate change. In the 1970s the U.S. Congress passed the Clean Air Act, which regulates "any air pollutants" that "may endanger health or welfare," including those that affect "weather" or "climate." This is the ultimate legal basis in the United States for the new regulations on emissions being demanded by those who sued the federal government to require the Environmental Protection Agency to enforce the Clean Air Act. The plaintiffs were twelve states, three cities, and thirteen environmental groups. In the United States, the early targets were smog and acid rain. Now the target is climate change. On April 2, 2007, the Supreme Court decided against the Bush Administration and for the states and environmental groups. Something like this fundamental environmental law should be enforced in China for all provinces.

Second, both governments should agree to offer partial financial support to the private sector for building carbon capture and storage plants, both pulverized coal and IGCC plants, and for testing underground storage. In the United States, the Department of Energy has been funding those, along with the private sector and some academic institutions, awarding US$1 billion in tax credits for nine advanced coal projects to which private investors also pledged amounts. However it withdrew support for the model IGCC plant (Futuregen) in January 2008.

Third, both governments can set standards for acceptable levels of carbon emissions for electricity plants. They can tax the excesses.

And they can let the market set prices for amounts of emissions. That opens the door for the trading of emissions among plants. Those plants that can reduce their emissions can sell unused allowances to others. There will be a market incentive to innovate. In China a danger is that some factory owners violate the spirit of the program, selling to foreign and Chinese brokers small emissions reductions for huge profits, to be shared with the brokers. The cap and trade model was successful in the United States with the control of acid rain. California has passed a bill that permits this trade, a model for other states, though opposed by many businesses. In Europe, the E.U. manages the trading of emissions allowances, and all countries participate. In the United States, this practice is private and voluntary. Where an individual state, such as California, takes a lead, it is likely to enact state laws different from those in other states that take the same initiative. Such variability will make it difficult for businesses to shape their business plans. I propose that the United States and China agree to follow the E.U. model of centralized policy, which promises higher standards and greater participation, and predictable rules on emissions from market trading of unused emissions.

Reciprocity builds trust. Other nations can benefit from China's experience with polygeneration. As Thomas Friedman has suggested, China could invest in U.S. companies that innovate in or already manufacture green energy equipment, especially in states hurt by globalization.[15] Then China could purchase such devices for use in Chinese factories, and increase its sale of emissions credits to foreign countries. Japan already buys some of those credits, with Mitsubishi as the broker. China can treat seriously its stated goals of a 10% increase in alternative energy use (solar, wind, biofuels) by 2020, and its agreement to a 20% reduction in energy consumption for each 1% of GDP gain, by 2010.

The United States can offer to invest in and share conservation technology with China, an offer stated by the Federal Reserve Chairman.[16] In a lead editorial, *The New York Times* recommended that this sharing technology applies especially to IGCC information.[17] The United States and China could also share in non-energy areas that produce global costs, such as diseases. Immunization and epidemiological technology are examples of mutually helpful zones of investment.

Reciprocity and Local Benefits

Potentially, reciprocity involves all the people of sharing countries both in immediate and short-term initiatives, not just the leaders who negotiate the long-term solutions. It underscores what local people can do now. Reciprocity can remind everyone that we are all in this together. Sharing the information they gain builds trust and spreads technology between the local groups.

Here is a typical example of this information sharing. In 2005 California hosted a gathering of hundreds of international leaders gathered in San Francisco for the United Nations World Environment Day. Among the guests were mayors from more than seventy cities from around the world. The governor laid out a plan to reduce California's greenhouse gas emissions to less than the 2000 levels in less than five years.[18] At such a forum, useful communications and relationships become established for common goals.

Within a few months of 141 countries ratifying the Kyoto Protocols, in the United States 132 American cities had taken steps to achieve the Kyoto mandated reductions. Almost half of U.S. citizens live where there are local recycling programs. At the local level, people comply not just because of material self-interest, but mainly because they agree with the morality of recycling or because neighbors do. Over half of the U.S. states have their own energy projects. And they are supplemented by successful NGO projects, such as the Nature Conservancy, that work with local officials and ordinary people. In China, the Nature Conservancy has helped people in rural Yunnan to harness methane gas from farm and human waste as fuel, reducing their need to cut timber.

In China, reciprocity should apply between local governments. Local people know that they may share in the common good if the efforts to control emissions and pollutants succeed. Allowing such an approach also helps nurture local democracy. There is already evidence from Zhejiang province, that, given information and a choice, local people will not choose to have chemical plants in their backyards but will choose sewage treatment plants and public parks instead. Stanford University political scientist James Fishkin helped a young party secretary in one locale carry out a polling of randomly chosen local people on which choice to support. They selected the environmentally friendly path.[19] A reciprocal benefit for the central government that comes from supporting the local activity is that they are likely to avoid a *tufa shijian* (suddenly occurring *local* incident), of which there were 58,000 in 2003, and 74,000 in 2004, and 87,000 in 2005.[20] A few hours down the road from the town that opted for a sewage plant and parks, an estimated 30,000 villagers had fought off police and established roadblocks to close down their polluting chemical plants. I would place confidence in what fully informed local areas have done and can do. To point to the successes of local areas does not absolve central governments from accountability.

Tapping Our Natural Tendency to Learn by Imitation

Humans from birth learn much by imitation. They are predisposed to copy. Chinese thinkers have known this ever since the pre-Qin period, when they acclaimed the teaching value of models for character emulation. The Italian neuroscientist Giacomo Rizzolatti discovered the neural circuitry involved in this process in 1991, agents called "mirror neurons." This discovery helps us to understand how we "read" the body language and even the states of minds of others (including models) as they pursue goals. These neurons facilitate both empathy for and imitation of another party. They activate the emotional part of the brain. We are beginning to understanding how successful behavioral change results from the presentation of a model for emulation.

We can apply these insights to climate change. We have available model people or organizations that exemplify prized moral traits in many places, and we imitate them. On the world scene one such a person is Wangare Maathai, who won the 2004 Nobel Prize. Kenya's foremost environmentalist, she has had great success encouraging farmers to plant green belts to stop soil erosion and create lumber and firewood.[21] That movement has spread to over thirty countries. Her message is that many wars are fought over resources, which become increasingly scarce. Looking to other and different models, we can appeal to photographers and artists to illustrate to the world's people what happens to our fellow humans when we damage our habitat.

In the United States, one set of environmental models is the governors of those states who joined together to sue the

Environmental Protection Agency for not enforcing laws controlling carbon emissions from power plants. They followed New York, which won a settlement requiring coal burning plants to comply with the Clear Air Act rules and reduce their emissions by up to 90%. The incentive to appear environmentally responsible has some motivational value.

China has its positive candidates too. On some issues it deserves international praise, such as for requiring stricter fuel efficiency on cars than is found in the United States (though less strict than in the European Union), and in producing mass transit systems, an area where the United States also lags behind. This praise is worth something at the level of international negotiations. We should also identify those in China responsible for specific innovations and give them public respect at the international level: those who laid out the incentives for Beijing's taxis to run on natural gas; those who designed porous pavement bricks using discarded coal ash, bricks that allow storm water to flow through them and go back down into the aquifer; and those who designed concrete blocks filled with insulation, giving warmth in winter and cool temperature in summer.

In both the United States and China, there is still timidity about appealing to the ethical principle of equal human worth and thus human health, in justifying measures to reduce climate change. In support of California's new bill to cut emissions, a prominent environmental supporter said, "This is not an act of altruism. This is an act of enlightened self-interest.... California will benefit its own economy...."[22] This sounds like the Chairman of General Electric in New York who said of his initiative to start designing clean coal plants, that he was doing it "not because it is trendy or moral, but because it will accelerate [economic growth]." The Chinese have usually justified improvements in energy conservation in terms of reducing dependence on foreign oil and on reducing air pollution (especially sulfur products).

What is wrong with these messages? They imply a fear of saying they support doing the morally right thing. Sure, they may think it makes economic sense to invest in clean coal. But the greatest impact of global warming, of bad hurricanes and rising sea levels, will be on the lives and health of our children and grandchildren, the value of the equal worth of all people, present and future.

This is a moral issue. Reference to it can only strengthen, not detract from, the economic case for going the road of the new technology. The economic argument for going the path of clean and renewable energy is that there is a lot of money to be made in the new technologies. But there is also the moral imperative: Protect the health of our children and grandchildren, whose lives have worth equal to our own. When the moral argument is added to the economic argument, we have an especially strong case for reducing global warming *now*.

Recently there were some rare but different voices in China. The vice-minister for environmental protection stated that his job was to educate, "so that officials don't just think about economic growth as GDP growth, but also factor in environmental health."[23] And near Changsha, in the town he has built, Zhang Yue, the founder of Broad Air Conditioning, told an interviewer:

> For years the Chinese government focused only on economic development, but now they say that the environment and the economy should both be stressed. But really the environment needs to be in first place, and economic growth in fourth....[24]

When a company buys a Zhang air conditioner, it also gets advice on how to reduce the need for it. Zhang has challenged mankind "to choose the establishment of the new moral ideal with higher standards."[25] These are the perspectives on which to build future negotiations.

Do we dare picture the day when the leaders of China and the United States, having decided to do the right thing about global warming, will themselves be recipients of a Nobel Prize for doing so? What fine models of character and intelligence they would be!

Appendix: Problem-Solving Models

China is not alone in also using what I call "problem-solving models." They are not the same as the exemplars of character and should only be imitated with great care, if at all. Do not confuse them. The trouble with the problem-solving models is that they are often applied to new complex situations different from the former situation that produced the model in the first place.

Once again, we learn from the new life sciences. Neurologists find that emotional signals are especially useful in social relationships where they help us avoid risks based on prior experience. We learn the body language of a cheater. However, at other times, the older, "reptilian" part of the brain wants, impulsively, to repeat what it has done in the past. It seeks automatic conformity to what gave the emotion of pleasure before. That reptilian brain in the people of pre-modern China loved the simplicity and symmetry of the well-field system. It helps to think that the reptilian brain intrudes into the zone of objective attention to a given contemporary problem. It intrudes into the prefrontal cortices activities, namely attention, memory, intelligence, and image making that are involved in reasoning. It is in these cases that the reflexive reliance on antecedent models can be dangerous.

There is a place for problem-solving models, but we must be careful. They must have certain characteristics. They should be compatible with the core values of a society. They should be changeable as conditions change. They should be open to competition from alternative models, and they should promote learning new technology. Chad Hansen has proposed leaders tolerating many alternative models.

Jared Diamond's book, *Collapse*, is largely devoted to societies that collapsed because they used the wrong models and refused to alter them. A dramatic example was the Norse settlement in Greenland. It adopted as its economic and cultural base the European model of dairy farming, rather than learning the more practical seal hunting from and trading with the local Inuit or Eskimos. In the long run, cows ruined the land, and the Norse starved.[26]

In China, Shanghai can at the same time be seen as both a great success in itself and a negative model. China has defined economic success as the first priority. Its planning consists of huge investment in highways, factories, and power plants. In 2004, such investment represented 45% of China's GDP. China modeled urban problem solving on Shanghai. Shanghai is an autonomous city that reports not to a provincial government but to Beijing. A former top official in Shanghai became the executive vice-mayor of the city of Chongqing in West China. Here, we can see what happens when such a model is followed blindly. First Sichuan was taken as a new model for all China.[27] In 1983 Chongqing was selected as the new model for economics in West China, and it was to copy the Shanghai model. In 2003 the leaders decided to spend US$200 billion there over the next decade.[28] There are under construction eight highways, two ring roads, eight bridges, and four rail lines. A Chongqing billboard slogan is "The way to prosperity is to build roads."

In following a problem-solving model one should not ignore but remain mindful of gaps between the model and the new situation. When the Shanghai model was constructed, China lacked a structured blueprint for environmental protection. Leaders of developing cities must now consider it as a priority. The Shanghai model autonomous city is not responsible for the impact of its policies on nearby towns and counties. Leaders of the developing cities need to think independently of the model and consider the environmental impact on neighboring areas. In solving its own energy needs, Chongqing should not ignore the consequences of its pollution on other places. Its waste water plants that fall below allowed standards harm neighboring rural areas.

Here is the consequence. In Tongliang, a small county about eighty miles from Chongqing, the agent for some improvement in the schools was not any Chinese local or national official, but it was Dr. Deliang Tang of Columbia University's School of Public Health. Currently the Shanghai model means that in nearby Tongliang, its coal burning energy facility has been able to emit pollutants that affect not only the people of Tongliang county but, perhaps, the rest of the world's population as well. The Shanghai model is also inconsistent with the core value of quality education for all, put forth by the State Council in 1995.

In contrast, using the reciprocity model, some Chongqing funds would be allocated to help Tongliang shift its coal burning electrical plant to natural gas and help retiring workers affected by the transition. Education on environmental issues would occur at the provincial and county level, even in high schools, sponsored by the central government which could phase out Columbia's Dr. Tang.[29] Then there would be more of an incentive for Tongliang to share its environmental findings with other communities. And the people would be polled to see if they wanted local funds devoted to paper mills and textile plants or to other non-polluting targets. With these steps in place, we would not expect to see many protest incidents in Tongliang county!

3

Application Two: Seeking Consistency in Chinese Ethics and Law

Useful Sources in Confucian Ideas of Trust and Shame

As an outsider who loves much of Chinese culture, I find in China today some profound inconsistencies both in personal ethics and in the legal system. In this case study, I will focus on the legal system, with a few words about ethics.

Inconsistencies

People who grew up before 1990 knew that they should prize above all service for others (*wei renmin fuwu*). But as they entered the 1990s, they learned that maximizing personal wealth was also fine. These two opposing values have led to shifting and often contradictory motivations among the people. Today students at New Asia College of The Chinese University of Hong Kong who wander by a lovely pool, set before a sweeping vista, will notice an inscription that proclaims, "Heaven and Humans Are One" (*tian ren heyi*). This message extols the values of a liberal education with its exposure to the varieties of human experience and to universal values. But those same students might also read an official Hong Kong publication that announces that the main purpose of higher education is to ensure the economic development of Hong Kong.[1] This viewpoint favors practical skill-based education that promotes economic growth. The former goal has something to do with character, with the values that can motivate doing the right thing as an individual as well as a citizen.

Returning to the Chinese mainland, one notes the prominence in traditional elite culture of the values of sincerity (*cheng*) and trust, as well as respect and shame-avoidance. Though these values remain a part of the culture, their importance has diminished. Once again, the result is inconsistency and confusion about acceptable moral conduct.

There are many reasons for this shift in values. For one thing, the public receives inconsistent official messages. A second reason is the mobility of the population, including the large numbers of rural people leaving villages to seek urban employment. If a person knows that he will not necessarily live next door to neighbors for a lifetime, the prospect of his being concerned about community shame or honor will be less. He can always move to a different place if shame is applied. Third, this shift in societal values also stems from the residual effect of the class struggles and Cultural Revolution denunciations of the Maoist years. These events undermined people's ability to engage in trusting relationships with one another. Fourth, the market economy often breaks the iron rice bowl. Long-standing bonds within a given enterprise may disappear if the enterprise changes ownership or control. As in the United States, it is easy for some employers to replace loyalty to workers with monetary rewards. Employees can now be fired regardless of their length of service and despite any prior promises. This situation coexists with back-door decisions in which personal relationships do count.

Judicial Inconsistencies

At the institutional level, China faces numerous barriers to efficiency and consistency, particularly in the legal system. One need only look at the training of judges to understand why. In 2002, a BBC report stated that more than two-thirds of China's 200,000 judges do not have a college degree.[2] Nor has there been a standard curriculum where they are trained. The government is trying to correct this problem: In 2004 the Supreme People's Court announced a massive program to train all judges in the coming three years.[3] And that same year lawyers, judges, and procurators were required to pass a rigorous unified bar exam. But sitting judges with questionable training were allowed to continue without taking the test, and of those who did attempt the exam, only 11% passed in 2004.[4]

The greatest obstacle to judicial reform is the fact that the judiciary is not an independent branch of government. Judges are government officials, and they are not appointed with life-time tenure. Local government and Party officials control appointments and promotions of judges, who then become indebted to them. As a result, local political influence can affect a judge's decisions. The upshot is loss of public trust.

Because Party control over the judiciary trumps most reform attempts, any systematic rehabilitation will come only when that control softens. A fair and effective legal system requires that the law and its application be consistent over a wide area of the country; furthermore, the same rules that apply today must also apply tomorrow. But this is not yet the case with law in China.

For example, in actuality, there are many secret or "internal" (*neibu*) rules applicable to foreign investment that exist in documents in an administrator's desk, but are not supposed to be known to the lawyers employed by the prospective investors.[5] Needless to say, foreign law firms try to discover and compile lists of what those rules are, so as to reduce surprise. In one such secret policy, an internal document drafted by the central government in Beijing told all district courts to reject cases involving land disputes. Secret committees may make the actual decisions of appellate courts, decisions in which political considerations are as important as the law.[6]

Another impediment to judicial consistency lies in the fact that regulations are formulated so vaguely that no one can predict how they will be interpreted by officials. One company discovered this when it learned of a law that supposedly blocked the sale of a company product locally, or approved it only for export. The wording of the law was so vague that in the end the company ignored it, without penalty. Adding to the confusion, case decisions are not publicized formally around the country, so information cannot be shared in many courts.

In the criminal justice system, lawyers are often hindered by constraints on what they may ask their clients and by the government's treatment of witnesses. Jerome Cohen wrote that

> [The lawyer, before an indictment is issued,] is usually not permitted to question his client about the facts of the case but can only introduce him to the elements of the charge and his rights under the law.... [Even when the investigation is completed] interviewing witnesses is dangerous because of the risk that a witness, under government pressure, may change

> his statement and the lawyer might then be charged with falsifying evidence.[7]

In the West this practice would violate the standards of evidence. Criminal lawyers in China must also contend with a bewildering array of conflicting laws, rules, and edicts. Cohen goes on to report:

> ... many conflicts between national and local norms, and the proliferation of regulations, interpretations and other edicts often produce incoherence and inconsistency.[8]

Prosecutors and community residents do experience some clarity and consistency in laws at the local level. But there are variations in how the law is applied from region to region and as a function of the social relationships of the parties involved. Though there are published codes of conduct, there are no national registries of criminal cases, by which consistency could be furthered.

In the area of business laws, consistency is often regarded with suspicion among local elites. While predictability may be sought by those with a long-term business plan, business owners often prefer not to have published laws that may prevent them from benefiting from future changes of the value of relevant properties. And once again, there are no national registries of civil cases, from which lawyers could extract even non-binding arguments to use across regions (The Supreme Court does publish opinions and "guidelines" for all courts and the defense bar.[9])

Public Discontent

The old value legacy that gave strength to consistency has lost some of its vitality at both the personal and institutional levels. The symptoms of this downturn have often been startlingly public. The government's failure to staunch corruption has led to frequent social uprisings. According to official statistics, there were 58,000 in 2003 (peasant demonstrations, factory strikes, and ethnic disturbances), 74,000 in 2004, and 87,000 in 2005.[10] China officially protects the "lawful rights" of workers and minorities. But the labels "lawful and unlawful" can be interpreted in inconsistent ways by courts and police. Even the top leaders sense an ethical vacuum and the need to promote a new ideology based on both seeking truth from facts (neo-

Confucianism and Marxism) and emulating Confucian ideas about a harmonious society.

I am not naïve about China's ability to overcome these obstacles. But it seems obvious that we should know what goals Chinese society ought to seek and how to get there. This is where the topic of the social emotions is relevant. Some of them constitute a relatively untapped source of motivational energy. This is especially true of the emotion trust and the emotional set of shame/respect.

What to Do

These emotions can serve as an underpinning for the kind of ethics and rule of law that are accepted as goals of the modern and civilized society. They offer an alternative to tolerating corruption. I will argue that any system that earns the people's trust tends to promote consistency in personal ethics and in law, thereby fostering stability. What roles do consistency and transparency play in such reforms? Together, they promote acceptance of the legal process and of ethical norms. With this acceptance comes cooperation by the public. In the absence of consistency, public attitudes toward the law suffer. Societies in which there is trust between leaders and people also tend to operate more efficiently. This is because officials at every level predictably follow the same set of rules and can make decisions without needing to consult their superiors for guidance at every turn.[11]

Thus the value of consistency is at the core of any healthy well-run society. Many Western cultures promote consistent (predictable) behavior through lessons in the home, schools, churches, or through news media. They treat this value as an essential part of the ideal culture in both law and personal ethics. George P. Fletcher, a professor of jurisprudence, has discussed how the popular model of scientific laws influences our thinking about a legal system's laws: "[T]he idea of law stands, more than anything, for inevitability. When a law applies, things cannot be otherwise; they conform to the law."[12] He continues:

> Rules connect straight lines. The same Latin root *regula* generates the words for rule in German as well as Romance languages. Decisions according to rules run in predictable, straight paths. Discretionary decisions invoke an image of unpredictable tangents.[13]

Transparency in the law is a recent idea that is closely linked to consistency. Like consistency, transparency leads to cooperation between leaders and citizens. It has few roots in traditional Chinese official culture. Even in the West, the popularity of the term is recent, probably deriving from the *glasnost* spirit that characterized the shift away from Soviet-style rule. But the idea of openness as a value in political culture has an earlier firm foundation in the democratic West. Any transparent system assumes the desirability of an educated electorate. It prizes the public availability ("freedom of information") of data about processes, rules, and participants. Advocates believe that such openness promotes public involvement in governance, including voting, and thereby enhances trust in it. As such, it is a non-coercive form of achieving cooperation in private and public life.

The modern Chinese term for transparency is *touming*, which suggests see-through glass. It is associated with clean, uncorrupt government and with reform. Transparency was not a value in traditional governance. To be sure, the public was interested in discovering details about what went on behind the scenes, and in knowing the reality behind appearances. But, until recently, the closest citizens could come to that value was in the notion of *gong*, meaning impartiality, or the avoidance of bias. Openness did not play a part in this traditional Chinese value.[14] I believe that transparency must join consistency as sources of cooperation in Chinese public life. When people engage in a cooperative relationship with their government (as with any human interaction), they can begin to experience a sense of trust.

It should be remembered that from the time of the earliest thinkers in China, human emotions, cognition, and motivation have always been regarded as being interwoven. This contrasts with the West's Platonic legacy that separated them into different, often mutually exclusive "faculties." In particular, I want to highlight the cognitive role in the two emotions: trust and shame. This cognition allows people to develop a system of standards and goals when they evaluate themselves and others. These standards can include consistency and its new companion, transparency.

Trust

Trust (*weituo, xinren, chengxin*) is both an emotion and a character trait. It is linked to consistency. The ultimate evolutionary reason people seek consistency is that it is associated with conformity to group rules, which in turn enhances cooperation. In this regard, natural selection works at the group and individual level. Cooperation fosters individual and group evolutionary survival and reproductive success. The proximate or immediate reason people seek predictability is that it is associated with stress reduction, as measured in part by levels of cortisol. Predictability helps people to feel in control of situations. This sense of power is both pleasurable and beneficial to health. Trust and consistency go together.

In its modern usage in the West, trust has recently been defined this way: It is "a psychological state comprising the intention to accept vulnerability based upon positive expectations of the intentions or behavior of another."[15] The vulnerability exists because the trusted party may try to derive some selfish advantage from the trustor without giving anything back. Trust comes when, for some reason, an individual disregards his vulnerability. Usually, this is because he believes in the integrity of the other, or he feels confident in the relationship that they have. This perceived integrity intensifies when the individual is granted access to information that will benefit him in some way; in other words, transparency builds trust.

There are new findings in the sciences about trust that can add dimensions to our understanding of it; but these supplements do not replace what we know from its earlier usages in China. The new findings include the following: First, there is empirical evidence that in one sense trust is a feeling. This comes from neuroscientific studies of those in a trust relationship revealing that the participants exhibit increased blood flow in the rear part of the brain that processes rewards. When a person recognizes that he is trusted by another person, his brain sends a signal which in turn causes an increase in the hormone oxytocin. The predisposition to trust and be trusted has a biological basis. It is a powerful tool awaiting use to promote cooperation. Second, in the public realm, people also give off *signals of trust,* to which it is wise to be alert. A possible cooperator may be out there. Herein lies part of the cognitive component of trust, the ability to recognize and respond to signals of trust. Third, as an emotion associated with certain values, trust influences our choices, making some choices more likely than others. Finally, there is some evidence for just what it takes to achieve a more predictable level of trust: the size of the benefit that the trustee expects eventually to receive, the duration of the relationship between the trustor and trustee, and, in some cases, even a person's body language or facial expression. For example, certain signals in one's demeanor may elicit in another person a rapid, intuitive trust, diminishing the role of calculations of benefits.

Another example of the new findings is in the field of neuroeconomics. This relatively new speciality examines how decisions about choice are made. Researchers find that humans are innately disposed to be conditional cooperators, to return trust if they themselves are trusted. So trust and cooperation are linked, for individuals as a matter of ethics and for institutions as a matter of law. Paul J. Zak writes:

> [N]ature has designed us to be conditional cooperators because it literally feels good. This positive feedback is how OT [the homone oxytocin] facilitates bonding of mother to child, spouses to each other, and, my experiments have shown, causes strangers who are shown tangible evidence of trust placed in them to temporarily attach to each other. The biological drive for social interaction requires trust and it is a powerful social emotion waiting to be employed.[16]

The experiments to which he refers include a "trust game." Subjects can earn money if they cooperate, but cannot communicate except by transferring money to one another through choices. In the game, the signal is a monetary sacrifice by one player. The right signals often lead to reciprocity.

My other source is Deepak Malhotra, a professor at the Harvard Business School. He also derives information from controlled two-person trust games. He has several findings relevant to this current topic. One is that the trustor and the party to be trusted have different viewpoints. The former focuses on the risks, while the trusted party is concerned more with the benefits of being trusted. The predictability of the trusted party reciprocating trust is in part a function of the benefits he or she perceives receiving from being trusted.[17] Malhotra's study also cites various studies that show that long-term relationships are extremely important in raising the probability level of reciprocal trusting behavior. He says:

> For example, in long-term relationships, people tend to stop calculating the risks and benefits that each party has incurred in any one exchange

> and instead adopt a more informal norm of providing, "what the other [person] needs, when it is needed."[18]

This insight is nothing new to those familiar with the trust bond in China, where there is a history of modeling relationships in the workplace on the family unit. These relationships have been widely torn apart since state enterprises started firing people in the early 1990s.

So trust is a universal emotion. Into its cognitive part can be built a belief that predictability and consistency are good things. In the pre-modern Confucian model, trust comes when one person sees consistency in another individual's words and deeds—behavior guided by the moral sense. Today, the judicial system can potentially foster a similar sense of trust. This relationship is dependent on how officials express—and act on—promised goals, processes, and standards of evaluation. In short, trust hinges on whether an official's actions match up with his stated policies. Transparency enters the picture when words and deeds are clearly stated and widely shared. The publication of court cases would be one way to provide transparency.

Shame and Pride

Among those emotions with a long history of prominence in social control almost everywhere, the set shame/pride (or respect, honor) also stands out. These are not just Chinese but, in part, also universal or innate. In a study of shame and pride among certain Malay speaking people in Sumatra, Daniel M. T. Fessler writes:

> The clues which displays [behavior associated with an emotion, such as eye focus and posture] provide are interpreted on the basis of *empathy*, the formation of an association between the Other's [another person's or other people's] display and the Ego's [the individual self's] memory of the subjective experience of the corresponding emotion. The ability to make this connection allows Ego to use introspection as a means of predicting how the Other's emotional state may lead to action.... Clearly, such predictive abilities are likely to be highly adaptive.[19]

Elsewhere, he remarks, "Viewed from a behavioral perspective, shame and pride became the foundation for a system of social control premised on conformity to cultural understanding."[20] Control is achieved by striving to elicit those emotions, such as pride and shame that reward conformity and punish its opposite. Individuals strive to conform to the expectations of people superior in the hierarchy, thereby permitting the inferiors to participate in cooperative tasks. Such cooperation has evolutionary value for all.

There are variations from one society to another regarding which culture emphasizes a particular social emotion. In some, the use of shame as a social control device is more pronounced than others. China is one of these. So I turn now to some Chinese perspectives on shame, which is, in effect, a potential management tool both within Chinese judicial organizations concerned with the law, and also outside them in the general population, in people's interpersonal relations.

The official public use of shame and honor has been inherited regularly up to the present at the local and national levels. I refer to the use of negative and positive models. Models exist not simply at the national level. There are local ones too. In Shenzhen, in December 2006, there was public shaming of alleged prostitutes and some pimps. Opponents said that those acts of shaming in turn had shamed all of Shenzhen, because legal acts in 1988 banned such public degrading.[21]

And if there is a desire to apply shame and honor as management tools, they can be applied in organizations concerned with the law. The cognitive dimension of shame (which rules were broken and how) can be available to photographers, artists, cartoonists, essayists, and public speakers. There can be public models of trustworthiness. Emotions are conveyed through pictures and words used to reinforce public engagement with the matter in question.

In a contemporary philosophical study of shame, the ethicist Allan Gibbard wrote, "A characteristic C is *shameful* just in case feeling shame over C is warranted on the part of the person whose characteristic it is, and disdain for having C is warranted on the part of others."[22] To "warrant" something pertains to knowledge of the relevant standards and facts about actions in question.

Originally, Chinese terms for shame (for example, *chi*) focused on publicly visible facts about a person. Another term pointed to something subjective, private; in the *Mencius*, that term was *xiu*, described as one of the four innate minds, the root of the virtue of righteousness.[23] The emphasis of *xiu* points to low regard for the self, caused by actions of another party. The *Mencius* has a story of a wife and concubine who feel shame when their husband begs for food from mourners at a cemetery.[24] The more socially derived idea comes from the *Analects*, that said when people are led by virtuous models and taught the rules of propriety, they will have a sense of shame and manifest it.[25] The inner source of shame does not seem to carry as much learned content.

Later these terms were combined in the phrase *xiuchi*, in which the emphasis is on looking at the self from the eye of other people, who may be morally condemning some visible trait or act. Also, the tilt toward an inner orientation is retained in the expression *xiukui*, which refers to a self-evaluation plus a subjective feeling of having some bad trait or having done some bad deed. Elements of both the inner and outer remain in its use today.

Let me turn briefly to some recent social science discoveries that provide clues about how the different elements may be related. Then I will return to the Confucian meaning of shame. The broad structure of shame as revealed in the pre-modern texts is consistent with that which emerges from the most recent social science investigations. For example, Daniel Fessler discovered what he calls the "logic of shame." It includes (his terminology): (1) Self violates a norm, (2) Self is aware of his failure, (3) Other person(s) are also aware of the Self's failure, (4) the Self is aware of the Other's knowledge, (5) the Other displays hostility and revulsion toward the Self, and (6) the Self experiences shame (*malu* in the Malay study group). So shame is a reaction to the way others feel about the self. Already prominent in this description is the fact that shame is not simply a feeling, but also has a strong cognitive component. This is knowledge of a social standard and of the fact that someone else knows he has violated that standard. As for the motivational component, Fessler finds that shame comes to be used as a tool to motivate people to cooperate with the group for goals that are beneficial to all. Turning to the opposite pole, when an individual tries to reform and discontinue previously negative behavior and do the right thing, his motive will involve the logic of pride (*bangga* in the Malay), with its own cognitive dimensions.[26]

These components are also found in Chinese sources' discussion of individual self cultivation and also of training by teachers, parents, and organizations. There is an internal component. This is the feeling, which involves sensing the self as below something else. It is not being tranquil.[27] Reference to tranquility has roots in such early descriptions of the virtuous person as this: "The man having *ren* rests in *ren*." And it is being without joy, because the righteous man finds that rightness gives joy to his heart just as meat does to his tastebuds.[28] Interestingly, in the late-imperial works, physical displays identical to those that social scientists and primatologists find in human and chimpanzee groups are also present: "...he dared not identify him, lowered his gaze, bowed his head and went away."[29] So there is an overt display of the feeling of "being below."

But there is also a place for the public component. This is the cognitive knowledge of moral standards of some kind, the basis for warranting shame/disdain, as I indicated in the *Analects* citation. These are standards with which the individual agrees (in the *Analects* case, the rules of propriety), and he may know that someone is beneath that standard, including, perhaps, himself. There may also be knowledge that other people look at the individual as having breached some standard (*xiuchi*). There is an implicit hierarchy image here, and the individual sees himself at the low end. The standards may be *yi*, that which is right, or some other principle. They do not have to be just the customary social practices of a community.

The earliest references to *chi* also include the motivation to do something about the situation, such as to leave a corrupt ruler.[30] The Confucian position was this: If the cognitive part exists, if it has been attained either through self-cultivation or through learning, then the feeling will drive a person to change, obstruct, or depart from that which he himself has disdained.

Our topic is what actions to take to instill the value of consistency. The cognitive dimensions of respect and of shame open the door to the teaching of consistency and transparency as values in political morality. Goals, processes, and standards of evaluation of official legal actions must accord with rules consistent with these values. Officials should perform those actions mindful of the rules of conduct that consistency and transparency impose. Shame/honor can serve as the sanctions for enforcing the inculcation of those values. In short, the presence or absence of practices that promote consistency should be the basis for honor or shame. Remember that the neurotransmitter serotonin evolved in us, among other reasons, to facilitate our adaptation to social hierarchies. Respect raises it, shame lowers it. Again, this is a powerful tool to employ as a social control tool.

Shame or pride can only be effectively elicited when this cognitive content of the emotions is filled in. In the case of individual ethics, it is a knowledge of a moral standard; in the law, it is of judicial standards. Whether it is a court in the United States or China, without a clear understanding about relevant goals, processes, standards of evidence, and moral standards, there can be a judgment of guilt against a citizen for non-compliance with a law, but there may be no shame by the accused person. There may be embarrassment in front of friends and neighbors, but there may be no shame. Without consistency and transparency, ethical and legal rules lose popular respect. They lose efficiency.

An Institutional Measure

I propose the reintroduction of consistency through trust as a value that characterizes the ideal judge. Shame and respect would be the emotions to be used to nurture this trust. The training method is by simulation, a form of learning for which our brain at birth has the right architecture. Cases taught by actual judges would illustrate examples of acceptable and non-acceptable variations in standard judicial process. Trainees copy their teachers. Hypothetical case models for their own solutions are derived from actual situations. Evaluations by instructors during the training program would use shame and respect to reinforce the students' grasp of consistency. The simulation approach is already in use in American medical schools, to train students' grasp of the standard of care in their diagnostic training. It is used in business schools, where simulated negotiating is practiced. Highly effective in comparison with other teaching methods, its success derives in part from the natural role of our mirror neurons in imitative learning. In 2004 the Supreme People's Court in China began a massive program to train all judges. At the end of the program comes a rigorous bar exam of lawyers, judges, and procurators in training. Initially, only 11.5% passed. This is the place to begin such training.

Appendix: What to Do? A Training Program

My comments concern maximizing consistency and its associate, transparency, in the judicial system. They focus on helping people learn to simulate actual situations in which they will make judicial decisions that advance (or obstruct) goals to which they have agreed. Simulation is acting and then creating solutions to problems within an artificial system that copies the appearance of a real-life one. This is a common training exercise in many professions. The Harvard Medical School now uses a mannequin, an electronic patient known as a "simulator" as an instrument on which medical school students practice diagnoses and treatments. The exercise includes built-in critical feedback or evaluation by faculty. Recent studies reveal that learning through simulations increases skill level to a greater degree than does any kind of apprenticeship or book-based training.[31] It is well known that pilots use simulators to practice flying under various conditions. Many courses in business schools, such as "Negotiations," are taught entirely as simulation exercises.

There is nothing unprecedented about ethics training for those in a justice system. The U.S. Department of Justice has a Departmental Ethics Office, the Justice Management Division of which provides an Ethics Training Program. It is available online at: http://www.usdoj.gov/jmd/ethics/

The training program that I envisage for China involves taking hypothetical legal cases for simulation. In the end the trainee imagines himself/herself being evaluated by instructors or other trainees. This assessment would be based on goals and standards that incorporate certain values approved by the training program. Among the values that should be inculcated as an internalized standard are the two which are fundamental to the success of any legal system: consistency and transparency. As applied to training in the law, this means simulating cases in which the individual seeks clarity about the law, seeks to share information about similar cases in other regions, and seeks to identify and deal with local biases.

Most important for predictability, participants in the Chinese ethical training program would learn that other people care about whether their motives include avoiding shame (for neglect of consistency) and seeking trustworthiness. This caring sets the approach apart from the mechanical enforcement of rules and laws.

The reaction of peers to what the individual does is a central concern; the nature of their caring is a powerful teaching and motivational device for future conduct.

The core content would describe, first, the *goals* of the program. These goals are knowing the following: the steps in the *process* of making a judicial decision; where flexibility is permitted; who may be consulted; how many cases are permitted in a given time; and what kind of court aid is available. Consistency or predictability must be built into the process, because these conditions produce in participants and observers a sense of procedural justice.

Second, the content should describe the *standards* that will be used to evaluate performance or outcomes. These standards incorporate the values to be internalized as essential requirements for public approval. Conformance leads to honor, violation to shame. These standards would include the following: (1) The outcome should promote social harmony and cooperation; (2) there should be correspondence between the stated words about the process and standards and those actually used in the evaluation of simulated decisions, so as to generate trust in the process; and (3) as needed, other considerations may apply, such as the bearing of outcomes on such goals as the protections of natural resources, economic growth, investment, and trade.

Finally, the content would include *evaluation sanctions*, applying shame or honor based on the outcomes. Initially honor and shame would be applied by the instructors. The long-term goal is to have the individual's internal moral sense apply them in the absence of other outside evaluators.

When a person finally emerges from training to begin an actual job, he continues to reflect on how others might evaluate his work. This self-evaluation is reflexive, internalized, part of the learned aspect of the moral sense. The mind is its own judge. As the Neo-Confucians knew long ago, there is always a place in daily activity for "reverential concentration" on one's goals and standards, and how well a person is doing to fulfill them in daily professional work. Today, more than ever before, we know how important to our own behavior is the knowledge that other people care about that too. People care if we are trustworthy, and they show us they honor that value through lasting respect and cooperation.

4

Experiences with Tang Junyi and His Legacy

*Interview by Cheung Chan-fai**

Date: October 18, 2006
Time: 10:00–12:00

Cheung = Cheung Chan-fai
Munro = Donald J. Munro

Cheung: It's our great honor to have you as our Tang Junyi Visiting Professor. Mr. Tang Junyi constitutes a very important part of our history, in which we all take pride. In fact we are the last generation to have the honor to hear Mr. Tang's lectures.

Munro: Maybe we are the last ones with visual memory of Mr. Tang.

Cheung: Exactly. The next generations are too young …

Munro: Yes, they are too young to know Mr. Tang physically, but the transmission of his ideas and method still goes on.

Cheung: Mr. Tang does deserve more recognition and must be put in a proper place in the history of the Chinese University. This is what I'd like to do before I retire. We will organize a fundraising campaign in 2007 for two

* Cheung Chan-fai is Chairman and Professor of the Department of Philosophy, The Chinese University of Hong Kong.

purposes: first, to make a bronze statue of Mr. Tang in commemoration of his contribution to New Asia College and to the Chinese University; and second, to support further academic researches on his thought.

Munro: I am so respectful of what you are doing. I will be supportive of you.

Cheung: Thank you very much.

We know that you were Mr. Tang's student during your stay in Hong Kong. We are interested to know about your personal experience with Mr. Tang, your impression of him, his influence on you, and if that has something to do with your later work in the United States.

Munro: So, we can gradually make a shift to my later work.

Cheung: Yes. We would like you to situate yourself back some forty years ago when you came here, and tell us your impression of Hong Kong, of New Asia College, and of Tang Junyi, etc. You are one of the best persons to share with us in this regard. Another possible man we can ask is William Theodore de Bary. He also pays great respect to Tang Junyi.

Munro: Yes, he does.

Cheung: When he came to the Department of Philosophy as the Tang Junyi Visiting Professor, he was too old to conduct a mini-course, so he just gave lectures. He was physically quite fragile, but he also insisted he would still be honored to come here as a Tang Junyi Visiting Professor.

Munro: I am so glad that he did.

Cheung: Let us start with your recollection of what you experienced.

Fascinated with Chinese Philosophical Studies: Munro's Acquaintance with Tang Junyi and Other Scholars

Munro: I came to Hong Kong in May 1962. I first went to Taipei in 1960 and had spent the first sixteen months there. In Taipei, I was a graduate student. I had done my coursework at Columbia University, after spending three and a half years as a naval officer. My first interest in Chinese philosophy developed when I was a naval officer, strangely, because in the Navy, officers, and sailors too, stand watches. I often stood the midnight watch which lasted from midnight until eight in the morning. For much of the time, there was nothing to do. You were there for emergencies. Sometimes there were emergencies. But for the rest of the time, there was nothing to do. The rule said you could only read educational materials. In other words, you cannot read popular magazines. So I read Feng Youlan's *History of Chinese Philosophy*, and I read it in the English version published by the Princeton University Press. I was astonished at the similarity between many of the topics of concern to pre-Qin philosophers on one hand, and the Greek and Roman philosophers on the other. This is what first stimulated me, and it was not simply that they were similar but they asked different questions of what they had identified. I think one of the main differences is that the Greek philosophers were interested in truth, and their image of what truth is came from the mathematician Euclid. Their view of truth came from geometry, which involved intuitive first principles, such as two things equal to the same thing are equal to each other. And from those intuitive first principles you can deduce all other knowledge and then end up with true statements. Well, Chinese philosophers, as far as I could tell and what I had read so far, were interested not so much in truth, though it was their concern (of course they knew what truth was)—not so much in truth, as in how does a proposition affect human behaviour. I mean for example, there is the idea of determinism or fate in popular religion in the ancient world. Some Greek thinkers would try to prove scientifically that everything is predetermined because of the natural laws of science. The Chinese identified *changdao*, "regularities." But they opposed the kind of fatalism that you find in some of the early Greek writers, because it means human beings do not have any responsibility, they do not have to do the right thing or work at doing the right thing, because everything is determined. That is the impact on human behaviour of any claim about fatalism. That was of interest to me. I mean, it was the kind of thing I got out of reading Feng Youlan during midnight watches in the Navy.

I graduated from Harvard in philosophy. And I went to Columbia. I had spent my first four years in philosophy (three as an undergraduate and one as a graduate student). Gradually, I was not satisfied with many of the works on Chinese thought because the authors did not know sinology. They knew philosophy, but they did not know how to read ancient texts. So I said to myself: I have four years of systematic philosophy training, now I must learn sinology. So I left the Philosophy Department at Columbia, where I had a fellowship, returned the fellowship, and joined the Department of Chinese and Japanese, also at Columbia, with de Bary as my teacher. There were only maybe two places in the United States where people could study Chinese philosophy seriously.

Cheung: So one is Columbia, the other ...?

Munro: Well, it shifted. At first, in the 1950s and 1960s the teaching at Hawaii was not satisfactory. Eventually that changed, and it became a distinguished place to study.

Cheung: How about Harvard?

Munro: In Harvard, there were some.

Cheung: Like Benjamin Schwartz?

Munro: Yes, Benjamin Schwartz was a young professor, when I was there. And I liked his courses, but he was in the History Department, not in Philosophy. I would say the other place that did it best at that time was Berkeley. For a while, Hu Shi was in Berkeley. And I applied to both

Berkeley and Columbia when I was in the Navy. I was accepted by both, but because of de Bary I went to Columbia.

That began my sinological training. When I finished coursework and doctoral examinations at Columbia, I was awarded a Ford Foundation Fellowship to go to Taipei. When I got to Taipei, there was no institutional way where I could study Chinese philosophy. I wanted to read texts, read the original philosophical texts with a senior scholar. So very fortunately I found someone almost immediately who could teach me. He, along with Tang Junyi, was one of my great teachers. He was a *wangye*, a member of the Aixinjueluo, the Manchu Imperial family. His name is Liu Yuyun. His own teacher was Kang Youwei. He had an orthodox training, and he passed it on to his students. He was very much in the Hanxue tradition. So he spent a great deal of time on textual evidence. He was flexible and not mechanical in following the Hanxue School, paying a great attention to early texts and the evidence in them, and what was fake and what was authentic in early texts. So, in those days, he did not have many Chinese students. Later he had hundreds. Now he is very famous. He is still alive in Taipei, aged about 101. Rich Chinese businessmen built an auditorium for him to lecture in every Saturday morning. In later years, he would lecture to hundreds of Chinese people and many Chinese students. But in my time, there were just a few Chinese students and a number of foreign students: some Vietnamese, a few Americans, and a few British. I think I spent two hours a day, three days a week with him reading the classics. So that was my textual background.

While I was there, I began to study a little bit of *jiaguwen* (oracle bones) just because I was intrigued by the discoveries about what was on the bones. Then I came to Hong Kong in May 1962. I had a western philosophy background. I had read original texts six hours a week and studied hard for each of those six hours with this *wangye*. And I suspect ... I have no memory about this. But I suspect, because de Bary was my Ph.D. adviser, I suspect he was the one who said I should get in touch with Tang Junyi. In any case, through some intermediaries, some Chinese friends, one of whom now teaches in Australia, an introduction with Tang Junyi was made, and he agreed to meet with me. I think it was three times a week.

The subject of almost all of the initial meetings was one topic with many different applications. The topic was: Does Chinese philosophy emerge from pre-philosophical religion? And the introduction to this topic Prof. Tang took was this: Let us first study what "Shangtian" or "Shangdi" orders the royal family to do (the kings or the senior officials of West Zhou, and later East Zhou). We should start collecting those things. It may be to cultivate *de*, "virtue"; it may be to treat people kindly; it may be to obey Shangdi's mandate to respect "my ancestors"; it may be to be loyal to the king. Gradually we could identify many of those.

And then the subject switched to look at what happened when philosophy emerges in China. What happens is the command to cultivate *de* and the command to be loyal do not come from outside, from "Shangtian" or "Shangdi." What happens is that they now come from the human heart. In other words, all of the commands that used to be external in the religious period now come out of the human heart. And, indeed, as he taught me, the human heart is conceived by many of the early philosophers as a ruler, as a commander that issues commands to the individual. I can remember he was referring to a term even found in the *Xunzi*: *tianjun*, "the heavenly ruler," similar to what Zhuangzi called *zhenjun*, "the true ruler." When Zhuangzi is describing the mind, the *changxin*, it is a kind of commander inside the person.

So gradually we studied different Confucian philosophers, with special attention to what the mind of the individual, as opposed to something external, commands, and what the nature of the mind is. And I think that the conclusion would be that the mind has several features, one of them is to issue commands to the individual, one of them is to have feeling, one of them is to have intuitions. So we read the sections of the *Mencius*, *Xunzi*, etc. I had read most of these works in Taipei when I studied with Liu. Then I read them with, and discussed with, Prof. Tang. So there would be textual bases for our interpretations.

Cheung: May I ask what language you spoke with Mr. Tang?

Munro: We spoke in Chinese, only in Chinese.

Cheung: But, Tang's Putonghua …

Munro: Very bad … very bad … very difficult!

Cheung: You must have had a very hard time. I also could not understand him in the first few months when I took his class.

Munro: It must have taken me several weeks before I gradually got used to his accent. But fortunately we were looking at books. And when he explained something, or when we talked about passages in the books, he could put his fingers at the *zi*, the word. So I could follow in that way.

But the other thing that was very nice … this goes into the personal experience topic. It was that he asked his student Li Du to give me additional instruction when there was anything about what Tang said that I was not clear. So Li Du came to where I lived for about two hours a week in addition. So I had three hours with Tang Junyi and maybe two hours with Li Du, in which I would clarify what I was learning. It was a double check. Li Du was very nice and helpful. At that time, I visited Tang Junyi in his office at New Asia. But Li Du …

Cheung: New Asia College was then in Kowloon.

Munro: The old New Asia.

Cheung: On Ma Tau Wai Road, Kowloon.

Munro: Yes, right. But I did not live or have an office there. I lived at the Mengshi Jiaoyu Jijinhui (the Mencius Educational Foundation), because there was no Chinese University.

Cheung: No, not yet.

Munro: The Jijinhui was a place where young scholars could work, and they had a small library. It was very convenient.

Cheung: Was it supported by American funding?

Munro: I think there was also some Chinese funding in there. There certainly was American funding.

I was there for three months: June, July, and August in 1962. I was working hard in those months, but I also took time to go hiking and swimming sometimes.

Gradually I became fascinated with what I was learning about the transition from the Shang and Zhou religion to Chinese philosophy. So I thought it was a clue as to one methodology I should use when I wrote up my material. And that was the methodology I used in my first book, *The Concept of Man in Early China.* I thought that I should have two types of source materials. One was obviously the texts which I had read in Taipei with Liu, and of which I had re-read parts with Tang Junyi. But the other part should be the pre-philosophical religious part. And for that I needed to learn how to read *jiaguwen* and some *jinwen* (bronze inscriptions). So I started then … let me say probably the last month and a half that I was here. I started meeting with a very famous professor at the University of Hong Kong who worked on *jinwen* and *jiaguwen.* And I cannot remember his name …

Cheung: From the Chinese Department? Is he Professor Jao Tsung-I?

Munro: Yes. It was forty years ago. I started studying and reading with him, both in *jiaguwen* and Western Zhou *jinwen.* Then I moved to Kyoto and continued that work in Japan. In Japan, I worked with a professor at Ritsumeikan

University. And I worked at the Institute of Humanistic Studies, Kyoto University, with a professor named Kaizuka Shigeki. The Japanese have a particular strength, which is that they are great index makers. And so if I wanted to find a guide to every occasion in which the expression *changdao* was used, immediately the Japanese would have an index. So that was one thing I got there, and the other thing was additional training in studying the oracle bones and bronze inscriptions. So that's kind of a summary of the background.

Cheung: How about your impression of Tang Junyi as a person?

Munro: Tang Junyi as a person was very warm and generous. His generosity in working with me is something that will stay with me all my life. I wanted to try to treat my students with the same concern and generosity of time. Tang Junyi was very patient, and that is important for the learner: to know that you are not asking a stupid question. He also taught me empathy. I mean, among the items in Tang Junyi's own personal philosophy that I learned, the most important thing was the importance of empathy, as something that solidifies human relationships. And, of course, he believed it had a transcendental origin. I have read your own article on the kinds of love. I find it fascinating. In your article on Tang's view of love, there are five kinds of love, being manifest in sexual love, and love of beauty and love of truth, and so forth. What he's talking about there is the transcendental source of love, manifest in the five kinds.

But I had become a naturalist in looking at Confucian ethics. Tang Junyi was not at all a naturalist, but he was flexible, he would listen to me. I could understand the beauty of his metaphysics. When I describe this, I can describe it by talking about *tian ren heyi.* If I had never had exposure with Mr. Tang, I would have taken it as a descriptive statement, saying that there may be some natural laws that we share with nature as a whole, gravity, chemistry laws, and things like that. Rather, what I got out of Tang Junyi about the unity of man and heaven was something emotional, having to do with empathy with something where there is a non-trivial issue at stake. That *tian ren heyi* requires you to have an aesthetic attitude and the caring attitude towards an object or toward *daziran* (nature). I can still accept that even though I don't accept his transcendental view of Heaven. I guess, I think, he would accept my flexible pluralism, although not agree with my naturalistic focus. If you learn empathy from somebody like him, it is different from just reading the words.

Cheung: Other than Tang Junyi, did you have any contact with people who taught at New Asia at that time?

Munro: Well, I had an introduction to Qian Mu. I was here briefly on my way to Taipei. I went to Taipei in 1960. I stopped in Hong Kong and spent maybe two weeks. And during that time, my Chinese friend who now teaches in Australia introduced me to Qian Mu. And I came out to Shatin, which was then a small village. I talked to him. I felt that I wanted to learn about his historical perspective that was not directly focused on the texts which I wanted to focus on. No, I did not have serious contact with other people. I did not want to dilute what I was doing.

Cheung: I think at that time it was very rare to have people from the West having a serious interest in Chinese philosophy.

Munro: Very rare, indeed. There were people who made contributions to resources, for example a man named Peter Boodberg at Berkeley. He was a great specialist in *yuyanxue*, "linguistics." He may never have written a book, but he wrote many very profound articles on some of the pre-Qin philosophical terms. And, in England, Angus Graham ... eventually I had a closer relation with Angus Graham ... but he was not part of my original training, except that I read his books. I did learn from D. C. Lau, who was helpful when I was doing my dissertation. I met him first in London.

Cheung: So after learning with Tang Junyi in Hong Kong, you went to Japan. And then you started your academic career?

Munro: Then I went home and became a *yinshi*, a hermit, for two years to write. I was living for a year and a half with my wife Ann's parents, and they found a room in their building which no one occupied. So I was in there at eight o'clock in the morning, and I came out of it for lunch and probably at six thirty in the evening. Yes, I was a real hermit in there.

Cheung: So when did you get your Chinese name? Who gave it to you?

Munro: Liu Yuyun gave it to me, because he figured that "Meng" sounds a little like Munro, and "Dan" from Zhou Gong is appropriate for someone interested in Confucianism whose personal name is "Donald." That is the origin of my Chinese name.

The Development of Chinese Philosophy

Cheung: So let us come back to your academic career. I think, up till now in America, the analytical tradition is still the dominating force in American universities, especially in philosophy departments. Chinese philosophy is not taught in philosophy departments, but in departments of religion or Asian studies. I still feel a prejudice against Chinese philosophy in the Western philosophical field. Particularly, recent publications like *Wittgenstein and the Future of Philosophy* by some MIT people are still stressing that everything is analytical philosophy, as if other philosophies are not philosophy at all. I can imagine that at the beginning, it should be very difficult for you to start a serious academic study in Chinese philosophy in your department.

Munro: I think your overall description applies to the 50s, 60s, 70s, and early 80s. But I do not think that it is a fair description today.

Cheung: I am glad to hear that.

Munro: Not today. More true in the past. Do you know who Charles L. Stevenson is, the main formulator of emotive ethics? He was a famous American analytical philosopher in ethics ... back in the 40s, 50s, and 60s. Here is my little story. My father, Thomas Munro, was in aesthetics, and his philosophical training came from John Dewey. His Ph.D. was under John Dewey. He was a museum curator as well as an aesthetician. One of my father's books was called *The Arts and Their Interrelations.* It is a large book, and has lots of concrete examples from the arts in Asia, and Europe, and Africa in it. This person Stevenson, a respected colleague and friend, was once in my house and picked up that book and looked at it. And he said, "Don, you really must know something if you are going to write a book like this." Forty years ago, that was an analytical philosopher talking. Analytical philosophers examined arguments and many did not seem to care about content. That was the way it was when I was a graduate student in philosophy. That's one reason I moved to the Department of Chinese and Japanese at Columbia. It was true when I went to Michigan in the 60s, it was true in the 70s, but by the 80s things were changing. Then a philosopher of science came out of a physics background. The people who teach ethics, such as Allan Gibbard and Peter Railton, know some of the sciences. They know the social sciences very well, so when they speak about ethics, they know what social scientists say about people who make moral rules in societies and how they use moral codes. The people in aesthetics know the art world. There was a shift into content.

It does not mean that the analytic method is gone. It remains part of what the philosophers do. But there are still differences. The Philosophy Department people told me that they have great difficulties in finding somebody to replace me, because I have both philosophical training and sinological training, and many of the people they interviewed have philosophical training but maybe only two years of Chinese. They do not have sinological training. So that's why there is such a conflict in hiring someone, a conflict between the Departments of Philosophy and Asian Languages. Asian Languages wants a sinologist, and Philosophy wants a philosopher with an analytic perspective. So that is the core of the problem.

But, you know, I am optimistic given the number of graduate students. There are Chinese philosophy programs in many universities now, certainly not all from the philosophy departments, but the people teaching them have some philosophical background and are using philosophical methodologies in teaching.

Did you meet Brook Ziporyn? He was here in the CUHK for the Conference on Wang Bi and Guo Xiang. You know, there are people like Brook Ziporyn, he is one of my former students. A brilliant sinologist, he teaches in the Department of Religion at Northwestern University, but he has some philosophical training. So one should not only look in philosophy departments.

Cheung: So you are optimistic about Chinese philosophy. Not just for the academic world, and not just for the United States, do you think that Chinese philosophy is playing a more important role in contemporary philosophy?

Munro: I think it can, when it is approached in a right way. If people doing Chinese philosophy do only a textual presentation, in other words, if they say Xunzi uses X type of argument and these Chinese terms on this page, that page, and maybe that page, then people in the audience who come from philosophy departments or other departments, or from an educated general public, are going to be bored. And they would say, "We don't want this, it is too boring! What do we care?" Languages and Cultures department people would say, "Oh! That is very interesting," because they know the texts. So a person has to present philosophical findings accessible to a broad audience. You must identify a human problem or question. This is not difficult for people in the Tang

Junyi heritage. Present the human problem. Do not just present the textual problem. That is not of interest to people outside of sinology.

Cheung: It does happen not only to Chinese philosophy, but also sometimes to Western philosophy too, especially the German philosophy. There has been a lot of textual analysis on the works of Hegel, Husserl and Heidegger. That might be useful for some experts, but not useful for constructing a meaningful philosophical dialog regarding issues of human concern.

The Concept of Man

Cheung: Let us talk about your three books on the Chinese concept of man. Definitely there is no one in the Western academic world who has done so much on this topic like you. And do you find that this concept of man is a kind of philosophical anthropology done for Chinese philosophy? What implications do you find for Chinese concepts of man in discussions of human nature in general?

Munro: There are two ways I can put that. One is what I teach my own students about the assumptions about human nature found in many Chinese and Western works and about being sensitive to the existence of those assumptions. My own students have gone out in many universities in Asia and in America. Another way of talking about this, practically, is about what impact it has on my own university and in other branches of learning. There, I think, the impact has been interesting. I have been invited for the past ten years to participate in faculty seminars run by people from biology and psychology and to give presentations. That has led to my serving on doctoral dissertations in other departments (for example, in psychology). When I read the works of these former students, now established scholars, and of other scholars in psychology and in psychiatry, I can see the impact of what they have learned about Chinese culture and cognition, views of human nature, and the Chinese treatment of mental activities. One of the leading psychologists at Berkeley is an example of that. His doctoral dissertation, on which I served, is widely read by psychologists in the United States and in China. I was also asked to write for a psychology journal.

Psychologists are interested in the influence of culture on how we know, and I can bring examples from the influences of Chinese culture on cognition to the discussion. One of the things that I was able to identify is the tendency in many Chinese writings to identify a polarity and then to seek a middle position that is somehow harmonious between the two poles. It is very different from the Heraclitean legacy in the West in which the principal emphasis is on the poles. In the Chinese case, the emphasis is on what will introduce a compromise or a harmony between the poles. Psychologists can draw on this work and talk about how in Chinese culture people are culturally trained to look for ways to avoid polarisation and rather to look for some conflict-avoiding middle-grounds. And Chinese texts discuss *zhong* ("middle") and *zhongyong* (the "middle-way"). We do not have comparable texts at the center of traditional Western philosophy.

Cheung: How about Aristotle's concept of "mean" in his *Ethics*?

Munro: Yes, that is true. I think you are right. But I do not think that it has the prominence that *zhongyong* has culturally in China.

The other things I can bring to those faculty seminars of biologists, psychologists, and primatologists (people studying apes and other mammals) are examples from the early Chinese texts of certain human social instincts and emotions. Today biologists and neuroscientists study these same activities using current technology. I can point to textual references in the early Chinese texts, such as the idea that morality begins in the parent-child relationship. *Xiao* (filial piety) is the root of *ren* (humanity, humaneness, benevolence). And I am able to give them examples from China on that. So the practical impact right now would be in the psychology field most directly.

The Tang Junyi Fellowship of the University of Michigan

Cheung: Let's go back to your Chinese philosophy, your latest work and your recent research.

We'd also like to know the background and the details about the establishment of the Tang Junyi Fellowship in Michigan, and the reaction of the department and the university towards such establishment.

Munro: Maybe I should start with that topic. There was great enthusiasm for my initial proposal in our Chinese studies centre, in the undergraduate college, and in the university. When I first established the Fellowship there were written documents signed by top college and university officers. I negotiated an agreement with the university in which I would give a certain amount of money, whereas the university would agree to try to match, and also the university would agree to give fellowships for a graduate student for a certain number of months in a year, with the university paying. Sometimes they would be teaching fellowships. However, almost all of the people who played a role when we made these written legal agreements changed jobs. One of them was the dean at the time, who went to the University of Toronto. The Vice-President for Development left and went to Columbia, and other officials who were enthusiastic about fundraising when I spoke of giving the money, didn't do anything. My successor as specialist in Chinese philosophy, who was supposed to be the immediate actor, was wonderful. He did a great deal, but then he left. So, great promises, but then the actors disappeared. There was nobody who was pursuing the matter. I made regular complaints, because I had already made initial gifts. The Philosophy and

Asian Languages and Cultures departments could not agree on candidates for the Chinese philosophy position.

But recently I have been working with a dean and assistant dean on the project honoring Tang Junyi. They want it to succeed. I have approved a new approach. This is to change the program into The Tang Junyi Visiting Scholar program, for short-term visits to the campus by scholars nominated by Philosophy, Asian Languages, The China Center, or Psychology.

Cheung: Your experience illustrates one point: Both you and I had personal contact with Tang Junyi; but for other people Tang was just another intellectual figure. They don't think they owe this particular man anything. To them the project was just another job they had to handle administratively. There was no passion in their work. As you said in your lecture, we can't merely rely on information about a person's contribution to so-called "knowledge" alone. Seldom will a person come up with the idea of erecting a statue of Spinoza after reading his work! Spinoza, Kierkegaard, and Kant are all great philosophers. But you don't have a personal relationship with them.

I think why we want to do something for Mr. Tang is, after all, we human beings need empathy. When I was a young student, Tang Junyi was very patient with me. I talked to him only twice, and he showed his concern for me, then just an ordinary student. His empathy and warmth have impressed me for a long time.

Munro: While drafting the agreement for the establishment of the Tang Scholar program with the University of Michigan, I insisted that they put a paragraph in the agreement. I'll describe it for you: "The University [of Michigan] formally agrees to widespread publicity inside and outside of the University about this Tang scholar," which means that it is the vehicle for making publicity about Tang Junyi and about what he has meant. So explaining to the public who Tang was, what he stands for is part of this now. I've already given them pictures, which are the same picture you use for his statue, plus examples of his calligraphy, and brief narratives about him.

Cheung: That's great. In fact Mr. Tang's wealth of knowledge and his devotion to nurturing people regardless of their background are equally impressive. No matter how busy he was, he was always willing to give his time to students. That's what I've learnt from him. As far as I can, I'll give my time to students.

Under the current university system, a lot of academics stay in a university merely for personal achievements, like doing research for a tenure position. But teachers like Tang Junyi and Mou Zongsan were truly devoted to teaching. They are first rate philosophers and scholars, as well as respectful teachers. I still remember how we students bowed to them! But this won't happen nowadays.

Of course, we all know the hardship they had endured during the early years of the establishment of New Asia College. The ideal and mission they harbored and treasured have also imposed great influence on us.

Comments on the Department of Philosophy, The Chinese University of Hong Kong

Cheung: Shall we talk about the work of our department? Can you give us some comments and advice on what our department is doing now?

Munro: I hope I have brought with me a letter I wrote to your predecessor, Kwan Tze-wan. I wrote him a letter in July, 2005. I knew that you had a number of analytic philosophers in your department, and I did not know if I could write papers for the Tang Visiting Professorship that got into applied ethics and even applied politics. I also was not sure if I could publicly talk about the Chinese legal system. Then I learned that Liu Xiaogan was going to come to the United States. So I could prepare early drafts for him to read, and ask his opinion about them. Also, I wrote to Kwan Tze-wan, saying: I don't know if your analytic philosophers find this acceptable. And I said I was trained in analytic philosophy, I know what it is. But it's not enough. And I gave him the reasons, very clearly laid out in my letter. I had hoped that he would discuss them with the faculty in general. I think I sent a copy of it to your department.

I think it's dangerous if analytic philosophers have too big of a veto. It represents a bias. They are so sure that they know what philosophy is. It's always as they define it. Well, you can define it in anyway you want, but I don't have to accept your definition of it. I'm always cautious and worried about their trying to impose their definitions on other members and other graduate students. At the same time, I am grateful for their contributions to many issues concerning language, precision of argument, and clarity in the meaning of terms we use.

Cheung: Our department has three "legs": Chinese philosophy, Continental philosophy, and analytic philosophy. However, in the last few years, analytic philosophy in our department has dwindled because a few people left and we still haven't found enough replacement. But we've always tried to maintain a balance.

Munro: I think your department is very strong in German and other forms of Continental philosophy. It is known around the world for its strength there. That is quite important to me because the background I come out of from the United States does not have certain specific strengths in twentieth-century thought on which the Germans and French focused. One such strength is on the "inner life," subjectivity. American pragmatism and some of the other schools are concerned with the scientific method in philosophy.

Cheung: In this respect, I would say this is due to the background of our predecessors Mou Zongsan, Tang Junyi and Lao Sze-kwang. They're all influenced by the German tradition, such as Kant, Hegel, etc.

Munro: I'm aware of that. It's fairly natural. When Dewey was first starting out, he was a Hegelian because that was the dominant philosophy in the nineteenth-century West. So it's perfectly natural that the Chinese elder philosophers would take that approach too. But when the American philosophers moved away from their German background, they left behind the attention to the subjective world that the Germans and French were so good at studying.

The analytic philosophers don't come out of the Hegelian background; they come out of a physics background. They want to remake philosophy in the model of physics. But the attempt failed. When I was a student at Harvard, the dominant theory of mind was B. F. Skinner's behaviorism. He also came out of the positivistic background of the 1930s in Germany.

Cheung: How come an absurd theory like Skinner's could dominate the world for so many years …

Munro: I think one of the reasons was because the major thinkers in psychology did not pay much attention to our inner life; they paid attention only to observable behavior. So they could ignore the human emotions all those decades, which they did. Skinner would say the inner life is nothing! Do you know that some political scientists are still influenced by behaviorism? That's why they pick such absurd topics to study. They think: A great topic is voting behavior of a small Texas town. Why pick it? Because you can go and count the vote! It is interesting that one does not find many Freudians in psychology departments anymore, either, but Freud is regularly taught in literature and art courses.

Cheung: In general, our curriculum must be comprehensive, but our research must be focused. We believe in academic autonomy and can't force our colleagues to do certain kinds of research. But we always emphasize that philosophy should not be kept in the ivory tower. If philosophy is away from life, it's just an intellectual game. It's meaningless.

Another issue is the purpose and meaning of undergraduate philosophy education in present days: It's wrong to think that every student coming to study philosophy should just focus on research and earn a Ph.D. degree. The over-specialization of philosophy as a discipline is just wrong. We should not merely focus on one area of study and become ignorant and arrogant.

Munro: One thing I have observed is that you have a wonderful team. It appears not only in how the faculty members think and present their ideas, but also in the friendly, congenial way they interact with students. I regard this as an experience in which I learn much.

Munro's Recent Political Involvement

Cheung: Lastly, can you make a comment on your latest political involvement?

Munro: I'm not religious, but I've joined the Interfaith Partnership for Political Action (IPPA), an organization promoting humanistic values in public policy. Here I would like to read you a paragraph from our statement: "We advocate for a simple but powerful idea: That policies rooted in our shared human principles serve us better than policies based only on a purely economic model that says material success alone is the best measure of human happiness and well-being. Ethical commitment provides a framework for security and using material resources wisely. We favor using moral guidance to inform the standard economic model," and so forth. What I have learned from the Chinese philosophical tradition, and from Tang too, is that ethics often needs to guide social policy, and not the other way around, where politics determines what is right or wrong. IPPA is a political organization. We have been active traveling around and appearing in town meetings in Michigan to convey this idea, with respect to current social issues. Part of my motivation in saying that ethics often needs to guide policy comes from my exposure to the Chinese tradition, and also from a friend who himself was deeply into the corporate world. So I've moved from personal ethics to political action too.

Cheung: Your love for Chinese culture and your concern for humanistic issues are truly admirable. Again, thank you very much for coming to the Chinese University.

Munro: Thank you.

(transcribed by Lo Kwun-lam, edited by Esther Tsang)

5

Challenges and Arguments

*Interview by Liu Xiaogan**

Date: November 2, 2006
Time: 09:30–12:30

Liu = Liu Xiaogan
Munro = Donald J. Munro

Liu: Thank you for coming to our Department.

Munro: I am honored to be here.

Liu: In this interview I would like to know your opinions and analysis about general issues in Chinese philosophical studies and methodological issues, especially for our discipline, our field, and also for the younger generation, giving them some guidelines and suggestions. I hope I can publish it in our journal in English or in Chinese or in both.

Philosophy and Natural Science: Are They Mutually Exclusive?

Liu: Let us begin with your latest book, *A Chinese Ethics for the New Century.*[1]

* Liu Xiaogan is Professor in the Department of Philosophy, and the Director of the Research Centre for Chinese Philosophy and Culture, The Chinese University of Hong Kong.

In recent years you have introduced the findings of evolutionary psychology and the neurosciences to support two of your beliefs: those findings are relevant to contemporary ethics, and also so are Confucian theories about kin-centered relationships. You go on from there and construct "two-realm (or two-tier) utilitarianism." But some philosophers are worried that natural science will further dominate the field of philosophy. And it happened. After the emergence of Newton's physics, metaphysics was attacked in Western philosophical studies. Then the sciences, especially physics, took over some topics from the field of traditional metaphysics. And now my colleagues are worried about that. Should science take up more territory from philosophical studies? What is your response to this kind of worry?

Munro: My response is to ask who feels this threat, and I will answer my own question. I think that many of those who believe that drawing facts from new science is a threat are in the analytic methodology field. And my answer to them is they have many contributions to offer, in terms of making us aware of the importance of precise argument, consistency, clarity of meaning of the terms that we use, and many issues concerning language. These are all very positive contributions of analytic philosophers. At the same time, they have a narrow definition of philosophy or narrow assumptions about what it is. They made these themselves. That school emerged in the 1930s, especially as part of what is called the Vienna School or logical positivism. Their model was physics, and they wanted philosophy to be as open to precision as is physics.

I believe that philosophy and physics are very different fields, and although philosophy may draw on physics and on its methodology, there is far more to philosophy than what the positivists or the analytic philosophers think about. As for their narrow definition of philosophy, they ignore the entire 2,500 year history of philosophy in the West from the Greeks down to the present day, and in countries like China. The Greeks drew on all existing knowledge. Plato drew on the pre-Socratics, such as Heraclites and Parmenides; he also drew on the scientific observations of the day which you can see in his dialogue *Timaeus.* And he certainly drew on the mathematics of the day. One of his models was Euclid, from whom we derive in part the idea that the basic truths are intuitive, and we deduce the others from them in a mathematical way. Well, from that time, and in my own country during much of the nineteenth and twentieth centuries, philosophy was equally broad, often drawing on other fields. For example, William James, one of the founders of pragmatism, was a psychologist who was trained as a psychologist. John Dewey was trained as a psychologist and as a philosopher both. So what I am saying with these examples is that, if the analytic philosophers want to define the field of philosophy very narrowly, and feel threatened by scientific facts, that's their business. But no one else in the world has to accept their position. They can define philosophy, if they want, as the art of tying shoelaces. But nobody has to pay any attention to it. So that is my position. I would simply say: Who cares what you think? Take a narrow sense, but I do not have to buy it.

Now, we go from the critique of those who feel threatened to a more positive position: Part of what I do in drawing on the most recent cognitive sciences, evolutionary biology, and evolutionary psychology already has an established category in ethics. It is called "meta-ethics." Meta-ethics, among other things, deals with the characteristics of moral choice, moral attitudes, moral intuitions, and moral properties. That probably encompasses at least 50% of what I do. So there is nothing bizarre about doing meta-ethics. What I do in addition to standard meta-ethics is some evaluations in terms of a commonplace type of ethics—normative ethics. I am what is called an ethical naturalist. An ethical naturalist believes that there are objective moral properties.

Liu: You said that you are an ethical naturalist. Do you mean that you are so since your early study when you wrote your book or in recent years?

Munro: No, I am referring only to the book, *A Chinese Ethics for the New Century*, and to the book derived from my Tang Visiting Professorship.

Liu: I see.

Munro: I do not believe that I can apply factual information without having an ethical standard. And my ethical standard is what you correctly called "two-realm utilitarianism." It is that which permits me to make normative judgments. For me, that standard has been influenced by information from neuroscience, biology, cognitive psychology, and philosophical Confucianism. So in the end I cover two grounds: meta-ethics, and I venture into the evaluative realm, when I discuss my standard, two-realm utilitarianism.

The final thing that I would say is philosophers will never lose their importance because they ask the questions important to human life. Most physicists or natural scientists do not have the interest or training to know what those important questions are, because as individuals they are very narrowly focused, often only in subfields of their own scientific disciplines. Philosophy, if done right, may draw on all relevant available knowledge. So it is synthetic to some degree.

Liu: When you quote certain scientific findings to support philosophical arguments or positions, there are always counter-examples to argue against them. How do you deal with this problem?

Munro: True. It is not difficult to find support for the topics I deal with. I rely on probability. In what direction is most of the evidence pointing? If most of that is pointing in a certain direction, then I have no problem referring to it. I also draw the information from a variety of scientific disciplines. Some of it comes from experimental psychology. I would mention especially the study of early childhood, which is one of the times when children begin to develop language, and one of the times when they begin to reveal a knowledge of such ethical ideas as fairness. Some of these psychological studies deal with identical twins who are raised in different homes, and if you get, say, several hundred samples of identical twins whose genomes are identical, you might find amazing similarities in IQ or personality. Then you are permitted, I think, to make some comments about biological evidence or a genetic basis for your claim.

In addition to those fields, I also draw evidence from primatologists, from people who study non-human mammals such as apes and chimpanzees. And there are also people who study birds and fish. For example, the idea of reciprocal altruism, can be studied in fish and in birds—birds making warning calls save their genetic relatives, but by going out in the open and making a call, those birds expose themselves to a predator which may come down and kill them. But the saved birds and their offspring may contain the warning bird's genes, and they, in turn, may warn future members of the flock.

People who draw on scientific facts to deal with traditional terms like altruism, for years have studied experiments in all these fields. I would give you one reference. The famous article by Robert Trivers, "On the Evolution of Reciprocal Altruism," which was published in the *Quarterly Review of Biology* 46 (1971), takes that approach. So I guess that that would be my reply. The evidence comes from many different fields, namely psychology, cognitive sciences, people who study fish and birds, plus people who study specific subfields of psychology (e.g. early childhood).

Liu: As someone may say, there is also the gene making people act selfishly. It is in a certain sense against evolution.

Munro: Well, I think that people are drawing on a

misinterpretation of Richard Dawkins, who wrote a famous book, which has as its title "The Selfish Gene." The book is unclear what the implications are of his statement that "the gene is a selfish machine, programmed to do whatever is best for its genes as a whole."[2] So it took some other people to criticize him and clarify the matter. I think that the generally accepted position today, including the position accepted by Dawkins, is not that humans are entirely genetically greedy or selfish; there are many competing innate drives. But it is that, starting with the genes in the person, the genes are in the cells trying to reproduce themselves. So individual genes would make cooperative arrangements with other genes if that strengthens them. The genes in the cells try to survive and reproduce themselves, so they make contacts with other genes and form teams. Many genes form in a team. And the individual cells will try to survive and reproduce themselves. And from cells, now you get into complex molecular behavior. That goes on below our level of consciousness. So I think the "selfish gene," beginning with the tiniest parts of our body, refers to the attempt of the parts to preserve themselves, rather than to what we would describe as selfish or greedy conscious behavior. That line would be a misinterpretation.

Liu: Thank you. I would still like to ask you about one of Xunzi's theories. According to Xunzi's theory of natural tendency, when you are hungry, you want first to eat, but you do not, because you are taught to respect elders and parents. So morality is something learned, not innate. What is your response to this scenario from your ethical-naturalist position?

Munro: Well, my response is that Xunzi's position, I think, is more complex than the popular view of it. The popular view of it is that the human nature is all evil, meaning that it has all negative desires. I have written an article in a book, edited by P. J. Ivanhoe entitled *Chinese Language, Thought, and Culture: Nivison and His Critics.*[3] My article tries to identify the passages in *Xunzi* in which he also accepts that there are instinctive desires, and also there is instinctive interest in propriety (*yi*). My article rejects the popular view that Xunzi has no idea of innate instincts or moral behavior.

I could probably give you a reference. It is in the chapter "Wang Zhi" ("The Kingly Way").[4] The reference is in my book, *The Concept of Man in Early China*,[5] page 71, note 83. There is another relevant discussion in *Xunzi* chapter 5 ("Feixiang," "Against Judging Character from Physical Features"). There he says that what really makes a human a human is his ability to make distinctions, which can be discovered in social role divisions (*fen*) and standards (*fa*). I believe these correspond to distinctions in Nature. There is an opposing article written by Eric Hutton in the Ivanhoe volume. Hutton challenges some of my comments. So, in other words, I think the idea of innate instincts about *yi* can be found in both Mengzi and Xunzi.

"Imperial Style of Inquiry"

Liu: Now, about your other recent book, *The Imperial Style of Inquiry in Twentieth-Century China*,[6] there is a new term "imperial style of inquiry." To me it is quite significant because it is different from traditional epistemological terms. I think you do that on purpose to avoid misleading propositional terms.

Munro: Exactly.

Liu: And would you say more about your consideration? Did you find this term, or create this new term, or perhaps both? In a certain sense you created this term.

Munro: Yes, I did. My justification has two parts to it. The first part is that my term "imperial style" refers to the style of inquiry approved in the Zhu Xi tradition. And I thought it was legitimate to use "imperial" because the Zhu Xi or Cheng-Zhu School's approach to the classics was orthodox for the imperial examination system, and for the curriculum in schools approved by the government. That was quite true even in the nineteenth century when the leaders of the Anti–Tai Ping Reformation were associated with the Cheng-Zhu School. So, that is why I thought it was legitimate. The approach of the Zhu Xi School was taught in the official examinations and in the official curriculum. That is why I called it "imperial." It had the stamp of approval.

The other reason is that the more I studied the epistemology in the twentieth-century figures in China, the more I found that what they were doing was political epistemology. Not always, but often. And political epistemology has a somewhat different explicit motivation from traditional Western epistemology. Traditional epistemology is interested, first of all, in what knowledge is, what the origin of knowledge is, what the standard of truth and falsity is, and questions like that. It seemed to me that political epistemology is interested in what the interests of people are, including groups of people who can be served by a certain epistemological theory. As an example, I would say that focus on the importance of rectifying the mind and on the importance of innate truths can appear in both Zhu Xi and Wang Yangming as *liangzhi.* This serves a certain group of people. It serves the officials and the philosophers who are educators, because it says that they, as educators, have prior knowledge of truth since they already have been able to have the insights and have the intuitions. And that elevates their positions as teachers and possibly also as people interested in a certain political party. It elevates the positions of the teachers, educators, whether they are in universities, or in schools, or in the ministry of education.

I think that helps explain why some of the people who are used in the book as examples are politicians, and some of them are philosophers—philosophers would include Liang Shuming and Xiong Shili, but I also refer to Sun Yat-sen, Jiang Jieshi ("Chiang Kai-shek"), and Jiang Jieshi's Minister of Education, Chen Lifu. I mean, all of them had an interest in changing the minds of people first, and that is the quick way to unify politically and to promote a new China. They believed it is faster than the gradual economic transformation of China.

So I see that there was partially a political interest being served by epistemological ideas.

Liu: There are theoretical differences from the traditional epistemological terms, yet you still used the word "epistemology." Would you say that?

Munro: It does not mean that everything is different. I recognize that on matters about knowledge, there is a long legacy in Confucianism which starts in the Pre-Qin. It draws on Chinese Buddhism, on Weishi ("consciousness-only") and Tiantai Buddhism. And that helps to provide inspiration to Zhu Xi's school and to Wang Yangming. All of that is inherited in the tradition (not simply the political motivation that I suggest is present in the twentieth century writers). And much of that can stand on its own feet. I am trying to say that there is something more than the well known content in the last century's Confucianism.

On the first page of *The Imperial Style of Inquiry*, in the first and second paragraphs, one can find the position that "everything in the universe is part of a coherent, internally structured totality." And I say that originally "this idea helped to justify empire and central authority in the hands of the emperor, who keeps the whole harmonious." But I think the idea that post-imperial leaders in the twentieth century could keep the whole harmonious endures as well. Sun Yet-sen and Jiang Jieshi both hoped to do that. And the principle goal that comes from Beijing today is that the leaders would create a harmonious society. Well, the early idea of totalism, "all is part of the coherent, internally structured whole," continues. And I think there are some positive aspects to that idea. It makes us see that things are interdependent, which in some sense is true, certainly in biology.

Another thing that I mentioned is in the second paragraph on page one of *The Imperial Style of Inquiry*, "inquiry was to be guided by models, the legitimacy of which lies in the emperor's approval of them." And the emperor "serves as an ultimate authority on standards for understanding the whole." And the second part is "there are hierarchical relationships between the parts of the universe," and "the parts have purposes," leading them to understand "the good of the whole." And finally, the mind has internally a copy of the "orderly structure" that is outside the mind.

All of that can be found in Zhu Xi's teachings. But the ideas also have a political function.

Liu: So the critical difference between the imperial style of inquiry and that of traditional, Western epistemology is the avowed political concern or practical application.

Munro: That's right.

Liu: You also combine a study of traditional Chinese theories with practical issues in China today. I think that it is the feature of your work since your first book. How do you deal with the difficulty of tying together ideas across ancient and modern ages?

Munro: Yes, that is certainly true. I do that. Again, there are several reasons. One of them is that I do not believe that all wisdom and insights are new. To emphasize only the new is taking a suggestion from the commercial advertisements, in which the advertisers assume that no one will buy soap or cereal unless it is "new." Knowledge is not like that. Knowledge gradually accumulates, and we build on the efforts and wisdom of early generations. So because I do not believe that only modern people have important ideas, I am happy to go back and see if there are important insights as far back as the Pre-Qin. And I find that they do have very important insights. So

I would say, "Yes, maybe they are old, but they are also wise." So, it is one reason why I am open about this and believe in it.

Another reason I do it is because there has not been, in the West, any serious counterpart of state Confucianism, in which for long time periods the state adopts an ideology, the Confucian belief-system that lasts from Han Wudi into the early twentieth century (with the exception of the Six-Dynasties period and Buddhist, Daoist periods). To say this means that the central government maintains control over what the elites think. It does so by controlling what they must study if they want the privilege of wealth, and *guanxi*-connections for their family members. If you are a man or a boy and want that kind of fame, wealth, and protection for your family, it is a good idea to study for the examinations. The government, starting in the Northern Song also began to establish some government-run schools, and the government controlled the curriculum. At a later time, as in the Ming, even if the government was not paying for private schools, private schools (run by a lineage group, for example) often took as their model the curriculum in the state schools. So this means that there is some continuity of official teachings coming down with the government enforcement and reward systems. That means that each new generation of elites can have a memory of what the thinking was hundreds of years before. That is what I would call a vehicle or a transmission of early ideas or early texts down into the early twentieth century. If somebody says, "what is your proof for that legacy," I would once again say, just look at important twentieth century philosophical figures (except for Cai Yuanpei and Hu Shi); they are people who inherited a great deal of the Zhu Xi and Wang Yangming traditions, and they acknowledge it. Sun Yat-sen was a great admirer of Wang Yangming, so was Jiang Jieshi.

Liu: Can I take your position as to emphasize the continuity of cultural development?

Munro: Yes, though not exclusively.

Liu: But, according to my personal experience in modern China, in the twentieth century, the majority of cultural elites and intellectuals are attacking traditional culture. What are your comments on that?

Munro: I am going to exclude Hu Shi. I knew him personally. I met him when I was young, in Hawaii in 1958 or 1959 for two months. We were together at the same conference, and I saw him almost everyday. And my father had known him at Columbia. But I also saw him in Taipei, because he was living in Taipei when I was a graduate student. And I do not think that he had much praise for traditional Chinese philosophy with certain exceptions. He liked Mozi. In any case, I think he is an exception. Even the people who copied much from the West also inherited much of their tradition unconsciously.

For example, Sun Yat-sen borrows from Montesquieu's idea of separation of political powers, and draws heavily on the legacy of French political theory. But Sun Yat-sen was also a great admirer of Wang Yangming. Jiang Jieshi was a powerful critic of much in the West, but he had no problem borrowing Western science. He tried to import a lot of German scientists and technicians to China to help build certain kinds of factories. On the other hand, he always took the position of that rectifying the mind is the first priority, and nothing else would succeed unless the soldiers and the people have rectified minds. So I see them as having a mixture of Western ideas they accept, and Western ideas they criticize, and Chinese ideas they accept.

But Hu Shi is not popular any more. I think it is too bad. Most of the Chinese scholars I know treat him as an agent for foreign ideas coming into China and not really Chinese.

Liu: The issue is a bit complicated when we discuss the position of Hu Shi in China. According to Yu Ying-shih,

Hu Shi's contribution is not academic but to *sixiang jiefang*, the liberation of thought. According to some Chinese scholars or officials, Hu Shi's contribution is a bad one instead of historical progress.

Munro: I see nothing wrong in saying it is both. Some of the famous Chinese historians agreed with Hu Shi. I am thinking of the great ones in 1919, in 1920, like Gu Jiegang and people like that. And they were later criticized. There is no doubt that Hu Shi played a huge role in the Baihua Movement, but he also had a philosophical impact. If you look at the philosophy of education in China after Hu's teacher John Dewey came in 1920, you will find that their idea of "unifying learning and doing" by "unifying knowledge and action" is an important part of modern Chinese educational philosophy. I think it lasts, and even lasts in the Communist period, although they will never give Hu credit for it.

Liu: So is your position to emphasize continuity in historical movements?

Munro: That does not mean that there were no divergences. I am aware of all the important divergences. I would start by talking about Dai Zhen or Wang Fuzhi, for example.

Liu: Do you accept the term "discontinuity" for divergence?

Munro: Sure. Or new evidence, new values. Yes, certainly I accept that.

But one thing that I am getting into here is the fact that, for the past twenty years in the United States, the term "essentialism" has been employed like a weapon, like a sword, to cut down anyone who wants to talk about general properties. You and I have discussed this before. I am not an essentialist, but I am not somebody who rejects generalizations either. I have to emphasize that I know the exceptions in order to protect myself against the swords of the anti-essentialists. I know Dai Zhen, Wang Fuzhi, and all the others.

Liu: I think that China has suffered a lot from the two civil wars and the Japanese invasion, and many other critical moments. Many intellectuals suffered a lot after the Communist Party came into power. After the Cultural Revolution, many people, especially intellectuals like Lin Yusheng, thought that we suffered because we discontinued the Chinese cultural tradition of prizing social harmony or a unified morality. But some one said, oh, we suffered the Cultural Revolution because of the tradition. They said, Mao had launched a political movement, and China had a disaster because Mao carried over the tradition, like the patriarchic system or totalitarianism. What are your comments about the conflicting positions on the reasons or the causes of the sufferings and disasters in China caused by political movements? Some people say it is because of the tradition, others say it is because critics attack it too much.

Munro: First of all, that approach is too simple because it ignores the Japanese invasion, and the Japanese invasion made a huge difference to the fate of China from the mid-1930s onward. I do not think that there would be a Chinese Communist government in Beijing today if there had been no Japanese invasion. The Communists were very successful in mobilizing peasant discontent in the rural areas and turning the discontent into soldiers for their cause. In so doing, the Communists had a lot of skillful propaganda. For example, "the mass line" (*qunzhong luxian*), meant "we would always consult the people," and that gives the people the idea that the leaders are going to be very popularistic, grass-roots oriented, and democratic. But that mass line disappeared after the defeat of the Japanese and the Kuomintang (KMT), because the Red Army no longer needed food supplies or intelligence from the peasants. So they could stop having a close relationship with the people.

The second thing I would say is that scholarship can identify a distinction between state Confucianism and philosophical Confucianism. They are not the same. State Confucianism is exemplified by the kind of orthodoxy imposed by the first Ming emperor in which there is a very tight state control of what people think, and if you think wrongly, you will be killed and your family will be killed. And they treated loyalty to the emperor as the highest virtue. Philosophical Confucianism is not like that at all. If philosophical Confucianism has a supreme value, it would probably be *ren*. Such Confucians would draw heavily on the Mencian tradition. They would also remember the importance of the investigation of things, and involve Neo-Confucians like Zhu Xi and Wang Yangming. It seems to me what the early KMT government did, and then what the Communist government did, was to emulate state Confucianism as a totalitarian form of control of the minds and actions of the people. In terms of behavior, it praised the virtue of loyalty; in terms of thinking on major social issues, it praised the virtue of *dayitong*, everybody thinks the same as the Party decrees. And that is simply the opposite of good scientific thinking. Good scientific thinking invites many different perspectives, because it knows that only with different perspectives will the best ones be available for people to accept or reject, and to learn from. So the implication from all of that is that it is important to identify what, in the long-term legacy, people rejected and what they did not reject.

Let me go back a little back to the previous discussion. I was in China in 1979 as co-leader of a semi-official delegation of officers in American teachers' organizations. I had a meeting with an official of the Ministry of Education. And I said that in the Ministry of Education you must be very careful when you switch away from the Maoist teachings. Going on a new road, you must be very careful that you do not leave the people with morally empty minds. This person said that this would never happen in China, they would always have a socialist ethics. But I think that it has happened in China. I think there is among some people a craving for something more than getting rich as a standard of what is right. So it seems to me that there is still a vacuum in China. I am not sure if it will be completely changed until the nature of Party rule evolves. There are very good signs. China does have a legal system, though an imperfect one. It's just a slow process.

On "Guoxue"

Liu: I recognize that I have asked divergent questions. But I am still interested in asking one more question. I was asked by a newspaper to say something about the current debate about the so-called Guoxue. It seems that it is not easy to find an English equivalent for that. (Munro: Maybe "National Scholarship," or "Scholarship devoted to the country," or something like that?) Nowadays, we have in China a Guoxue Yanjiusuo, in Renmin University of China a Guoxue Yuan, in *Guangming Ribao* a Guoxue page, and on the internet some Guoxue Wang, webs on Guoxue. Some scholars promote the Gongyang political philosophy, some promote the *Sanzijing* or even the *Dizigui*, the rule for disciples. So many intellectuals are worried and they criticize this so-called "Guoxuere" (fad for Guoxue), but others promote Guoxue. So they asked me to say something about that. It is quite difficult. The same issue was dealt with a hundred years ago in the May Fourth Movement as in whether people should defend or promote traditional culture. As for the term "Guoxue," I think it is a complicated issue. But I think it has come again and again. The essential question is how we should treat our cultural tradition, especially Confucianism and Daoism and Buddhism. I think the core of Guoxue is Confucianism and Daoism and Buddhism, and not literature and music and art. What are your comments on this debate about Guoxue?

Munro: This is a new question for me. My initial reaction to this is that Guoxue has a very important role in any country, especially in supporting patriotism that is essential for national protection. People in any country have the right to protect themselves. Patriotism can be nurtured by Guoxue. I think it is legitimate and necessary. Of course, that would include the study of things that Chinese people share.

I would disagree with you on the elimination of art and paintings. I found that many Chinese paintings are intimately connected to the philosophical positions that you mentioned. I think that they serve to carry on the emotional importance of some of the philosophical ideas. When you see a kind of standard landscape with a tiny person in the hut, and a huge mountain inspired by Guilin, you get an idea of *tian ren heyi*, which is a philosophical idea.

It seems to me that the second reason for Guoxue is to alert people to the treasures that are part of the culture. Nobody can know about these treasures unless people of their generation write about them or museum curators send exhibits around the country. That is why the Shanghai Historical Museum is fabulous, and it is important not only for world culture, but it is important for Chinese unity, so the Chinese people know that this is something Chinese people share.

But, having said those two things, I would say I hope that as we begin entering an era of global knowledge, an appreciation of the global, universal nature of humanity will emerge. We can start thinking about what is right and wrong for humanity, because we are now capable of sharing information electronically, and we are all affected by what happens in each other's country. For instance, pollutants in China affect the breathing of people in Los Angeles, and waste computers from abroad get dumped outside of Shanghai (though that became illegal in 2003). These are the things that affect both of our nations. So, part of my answer is that there are some things that are now part of the international discussion of ethics.

Liu: My position is that the core of Guoxue should be philosophy consisting of Confucianism, Daoism, and Buddhism. And I said that because I have just read an essay by a famous painter, Huang Yongyu. He does not like the term "Guoxue." Why should we have "Guohua," "Guoyue"? Why must we use the word *guo*? What we do is simply painting, and that is not to be classified as "Western" or "Chinese." I think it is just alright for painting; in painting, we do not have to keep the Chinese tradition.

Munro: Certainly I agree with what you have been expressing. The fact that one enters international dialogues does not mean abandoning one's own culture. We have skills and topics we regard as worthwhile, you do too. We can learn from each other.

I can identify elements of the Confucian tradition that are alive today, probably not very often publicized but are much alive, and worth preserving. I would mention the value placed on education, including education of children. This is concretely manifest in the amount of time that Chinese parents spend with their children, helping them with homework, trying to cultivate discipline, making sure they do their studies, going to the schools and participating there. It is far greater than I have observed anywhere else, and certainly greater than in the United States. And this is part of a philosophical legacy with Asian roots. It became part of the socialization process, it is a part of what one is taught as a child. It is carried on in the children's bedroom, and when some adults read philosophical works.

Another element would be *xiao* (filial piety). Obviously, in China today there can be economic reasons for emphasizing that. The government does not have to pay pensions. If they can say, it is your obligation to pay for the upkeep of your parents, then the state does not have to pay the money. But that is only part of it. Another part of it is also the fact that the love of parents is inborn and natural, and it appeals to innate emotions and intuitions.

On Intellectuals' Attitude toward Traditional Culture

Liu: Before I move on to Question Five, I still have a question to ask. I am curious about the attitude of Chinese intellectuals toward traditional culture. Quite a number of very outstanding intellectuals and scholars have a strong feeling against Chinese cultural tradition. I am curious about why it happened, and why it can last so long, for almost over a century. In contrast, the Jewish people have suffered for thousands of years. But criticizing their own cultural and religious tradition is not part of their mainstream. I wonder why the difference is so great between Chinese intellectuals and Jewish intellectuals.

A friend of mine is a Jewish psychologist. She holds a Ph.D. in psychology. She asks her 5-year-old boy to go to school every Sunday to study Hebrew. Studying Hebrew is not practical in the United States, but this is their tradition. And her family burns candles every Friday evening. She is not religious, but again it is a tradition. For scientists or intellectuals with a rational thinking, it does not make sense. For them, they just keep their tradition faithfully. But why do Chinese intellectuals criticize their tradition so easily and so strongly?

Munro: I think that there are some obvious candidates as explanation. One reason is that part of the Confucian tradition is identified with State Confucianism, and there have been abuses of that central power.

Also there can be criticism without much knowledge of what their cultural tradition is. When I talk to Chinese students, I find many have a minimal knowledge of their own cultural tradition. Let us think for a minute about some of the possible explanations for this.

People often learn what their leaders emphasize themselves. China's leaders for the past forty years (except for some Long March veterans) generally have been engineers. Engineers have a narrow education.

They do not have much knowledge of their own culture. It is true in the United States as well as in China. (Personal anecdote: my uncle was an engineer. He was very smart on engineering and mathematical issues, but not anything else. He had terrible opinions.) And now, what is occurring in China is a kind of "marriage" of leaders who are engineers, often graduated from Tsinghua University or Shanghai Telecommunications University, with financial people. The financial people often do not have any knowledge of their culture, unless they are very rich, and then they start to buy traditional Chinese artworks. So there is a huge educational gap about Chinese culture in China. Who is making the case for the importance of elements of the Chinese culture? Well, I am, but I am not a Chinese. There are people at this university. There are certainly other Chinese who do so abroad, outside of the mainland. Hopefully there are others in the mainland. But when you look at the Chinese curriculum, you are not going to find much of traditional culture. Before this marriage of engineers and financial people, the focus was "Ma-Lie" [Marxism-Leninism] and Chairman Mao's thought.

Liu: I think you have answered my question when you mentioned State Confucianism. People have a resentment to Confucianism because of this. Basically why they dislike Confucianism is because of the setting-in-force of Confucianism by the governments in the past. Perhaps that is one of the reasons. It has become an ideology. Yes, I think what you said has touched the essential part of my question. For the Jews, they keep the tradition voluntarily. But in China, Confucianism had become an ideology and thus a political issue.

Munro: I would say that it is. And my next comment after that would be to identify some of the positive inheritances. That is what I tried to do in *A Chinese Ethics for the New Century*. It is to identify some, such as the importance of an innate sense of sympathy and empathy, which are now scientifically studied.

The Use of Images: A New Methodological Approach

Liu: Your book, *Images of Human Nature*,[7] has a very new methodological approach. It is quite different from your first two books. I wonder how you found this approach. What happened to you when you shifted from the approaches in your first two books to this approach?

Munro: I think the beginning of it was that as soon as I finished my second book, *The Concept of Man in Contemporary China*, in 1978, I started doing readings in Zhu Xi's texts. So I had a little knowledge in those early years. At the same time, what I found out through biographical stories and also from readings in psychology and anthropology were two things. Firstly, there was evidence that certain people think more in pictures rather than in words. Some of the most famous mathematicians and Nobel physicists have explicitly stated that they think in pictures. On page 22 of my *Images of Human Nature: A Sung Portrait*, I mention that the mathematician S. M. Ulam wrote in his memoirs, "It is said that seventy-five percent of us have a dominant visual memory, twenty-five percent an auditory one. As for me, mine is quite visual. When I think about mathematical ideas, I see the abstract notions in symbolic pictures."[8] Then I quote from a famous British physicist, Freeman Dyson. "Dick [Feynmann] just wrote down the solutions out of his head without ever writing down the equations. He had a physical picture of the way things happen, and the picture gave him the solution directly, with a minimum of calculation. It was no wonder that people who had spent their lives solving equations were baffled by him. Their minds were analytical; his mind was pictorial."[9] He continued, "My own training, since the far off days when I struggled with H. Y. H. Piaggio's differential equations, had been analytical. But as I listened to Dick and stared at the strange diagrams that he drew on the blackboard I gradually absorbed some of his pictorial imagination and began to feel at home in his version of the universe."[10] I have indicated two physicists and one mathematician who say they think visually. There are also psychologists and anthropologists who have found that people think pictorially.

Secondly, there was one other thing that made a light go off in my head. When the light bulb went off, it said to me: Some people think in images; there is evidence for that. Now, consisder that Zhu Xi is constantly using pictures: water, tree, plant, the light, and all the other images I talked of in *Images of Human Nature.* This is especially true of the *Yu Lei* (*Classified Conversations*), because that is where he was being confronted by students who did not understand. In order to clarify, he used an image. The other thing that happened was that American people in linguistics started to write about metaphors. There is a famous linguistic specialist in Berkeley. His name is George Lakoff. He has written several influential books about how people use metaphors. So I was influenced by his early findings.

Liu: Do you think you can use the same method for the studies of Confucius and Mengzi?

Munro: Not necessarily, I do not know. I have to look into the details. A young colleague of mine believes he can do that and has written an important book supporting his view. I have great respect for him as a scholar.

Liu: Is he Edward Slingerland, who wrote a book on *wuwei*?[11] He used the metaphor theory. He said *wuwei* is the metaphor. I do not understand, because *wuwei* is not an image.

Munro: I agree that *wuwei* is not a metaphor or an image. Slingerland would agree that it is abstract. What he does is to focus on what he calls the "conceptual metaphors" that arise when our embodied mind reacts to the physical world. In this context, he said that when *wuwei* is the topic, there is often reference to the individual self and its lack of purposive control. So physical metaphors such as "following" (surrendering control) and "resting" are used. I think he does a good job when he argues like this.

But I have not tried myself to do this with the early Chinese texts. I do not know if it could be done for all of the classical philosophical texts. I would not infer that it is impossible. Some of Zhu Xi's use of metaphors, not all of them, but some of the important ones, come from Buddhists and Daoists. Daoists love to use the light imagery to talk about knowledge or insight or enlightenment. My method is dictated by the text, not in the other way round. We should first read the text, get a suggestion, and then go back and see if it's confirmed by the evidence in texts.

Liu: It seems to me that you used images as the structure of your research. But for Zhu Xi, the images are just the means. So what is the advantage of doing so?

Munro: The advantage comes from the fact that he has to rely on images when he is trying to explain to his students what is basic and what has priority, so that they clearly understand. That is why I focused on the *Yu Lei*. Almost all of my evidence comes from *Yu Lei*, because I found that the evidence of what he believed to be basic and core lies in how he explained his theory to students, that is using concrete or pictorial analogies. I discovered that in reading and comparing his different kinds of writing. So my claims are not necessarily applicable to his more theoretical things. Maybe they are, Maybe they aren't. But I made my case based on *Yu Lei*.

Philosophical versus Historical Approach

Liu: Do you know Willard Peterson? He said your book is more philosophical instead of being an intellectual history. What is your response to it?

Munro: Frankly speaking, a more accurate way of describing his review is that he has nothing nice to say. That is alright.

I do not understand the difference he refers to as between "philosophical" and "intellectual history." I understand what relying on evidence is. When I developed the hypothesis in the late 1970s, I spent nearly the next ten years reading Zhu Xi's works. There is the source of my evidence. And as evidence, I give the quotes to support my hypothesis about his use of images. In the little that I read of Peterson's work that had any relevance to the Cheng-Zhu School, the only thing I can say is this. He was not quick enough to understand the importance of imagistic thinking both as a Zhu Xi and as a human phenomenon.

To this day, the historians always attack me for not being a historian. They want me to write history, talking about social roots, currencies, and the economy of the period. If I did that, nobody would be interested in the ideas. So you have to make some choices. I have tried. I think I do give historical backgrounds in most of my books. But I cannot do it like a historian. So I will always be open to the historians' criticisms. They are saying, well, why aren't you a historian?

Liu: I think the field of so-called Chinese philosophy is somehow open to various perspectives. Anyone who studies literature, history, philosophy or linguistics can come in. Somehow it is good. We would have contributions from different disciplines. But sometimes they would just evaluate and criticize our work from certain narrow aspects.

Munro: If you ask me to think about modern interpretations and historical data, I think we should respect both approaches and learn from them both. I learn from the historians, and perhaps it is time for them to think that they can learn something from philosophers too.

Liu: I disagree with A. C. Graham's way of dealing with Zhuangzi or some other positions. But, in general, his interests are quite broad. He is a sinologist, a linguist, a philosopher, an all-rounded scholar.

Munro: I agree with that entirely.

On the Concept of "Clustering"

Liu: In your book, *The Concept of Man in Contemporary China,* you developed a new, critical concept, "clustering." Did you find this term or did you create this term?

Munro: I found the phenomenon first, and then I tried to find a term to express it. What I found was that during the period from early 1940s to 1976 the Chinese writers used a single psychological term with different contents. For instance, one such Chinese term is a term for "to know" *renshi.* They might use it in such a way that it highlighted "grasping facts," But at other times it stressed "emotional approval," and sometimes it indicated mainly a motive for action (because someone has *renshi,* therefore he acted). So it was this phenomenon of different but related meanings, all present but one highlighted, for the same technical term that led me to call the practice "clustering."

After doing that, I then found a similar phenomenon in Zhu Xi's works, which I was just beginning to look at. But all of that came after I identified this phenomenon in Chinese writings on *renxing* (human nature) and from psychology (I got the psychology materials in the journal *Xinli Xuebao* and articles from other journals). And wherever the articles were appearing on Chinese psychology, they were doing this. And there was no English term. So I simply called it "clustering."

Liu: That means you found the phenomena in modern China and in history. And you created the term.

Munro: Exactly. And, once again, to return to the topic of criticism we were talking about just now, one of the reviewers of that book said that I used too many jargon terms. I do not mind calling "clustering" a jargon term, if that does not detract from considering the nature of the practice. One thing I always try to teach my students is to look for the strengths in an article or position that you disagree with, because there may be positive findings even if you do not agree with the rest, or find its "jargon" distasteful.

Liu: I find that finding others' strengths is more useful than finding their shortcomings. It is more helpful for oneself and for the academic world as well. I agree with you.

Munro's Areas of Interest

Liu: I have a small question here. I am curious about why, after finishing that book, you jumped into the study of contemporary China instead of the Song dynasty?

Munro: Sometimes answers are very ordinary. A young scholar is dependent on middle-level and senior scholars. He is dependent for his job and for his evaluations. At that time in my life, I was still an untenured faculty member, and my seniors asked me to do two things. One was to teach Western political philosophy in the Philosophy Department. And the other was to teach, as part of a team, a course on "China's Evolution under Communism" in the college as a whole. The course was cross-listed in politics, economics, and philosophy. So I said, "Yes, Sir!" I obeyed, and I would teach these two. But I did not know much about political philosophy. So I had to read about it. And part of my readings included Marxism and Leninism. And in order to prepare to teach my part of "China's Evolution under Communism," I had to read Chinese Marxism and Leninism, starting from the 1920s up until that time which was late 1960s and 1970s. So that is why I focused on it.

I found that I could still deal with my main life topic, which is theories of human nature, but I also could fit it into learning about Chinese Marxism for my college duties. In the mid-1960s I spent a year in Hong Kong (with interviews also in Macau) doing some of the work on that project.

Liu: That is good. You followed the order, and you also created your own.

Interrelatedness of Knowledge, and Humanistic Concerns

Liu: Let us move on to your first book, *The Concept of Man in Early China.* In this book, again, did you perhaps find the phenomenon or the idea of "natural equality" and then create the term?

Munro: I did not create this term. It was used by an author of a book on equality that probably came out in the late 1950s or early 1960s. But it was not used much by many other authors. The term "natural equality" was used in that book to refer to ways in which people are factually similar. I thought that it was natural to apply it to what I had previously found in some of the Chinese works, which is: people are all equal in the sense that they all have the "four minds." That was natural equality too.

Liu: For me, a distinguished feature of your first book is that it is a good combination of a sinological approach and philosophical analysis. I think you did it perfectly. But for the younger generation, they want to publish books before they can combine sinology and philosophy.

So, some people may think that philosophical analysis, such as the approach of analytical philosophy or pragmatism, is perhaps not necessary for the study of Chinese philosophical texts. Other people may think that, well, we are philosophers, we read philosophical works, we philosophize on Confucian theories, we do not need to be historians or sinologists. So it seems that for them there are difficulties in combining philosophy and sinology. Some may think that it is not necessary or practical. Personally, I think it is good to combine them together. But it is so difficult to achieve the goal. What is your suggestion or opinion about that?

Munro: I agree with your position. I think to combine sinology and philosophy is the way I would always encourage my students to go. My answer to your question would be different if I were talking to American graduate students or Chinese graduate students. In the American case, I would say to them, you must get to the point where you can read the pre-Qin philosophers in the original *wenyan* editions, not relying on translations or other people's scholarship. That is how you may get close to the original meanings. You should take courses with someone either in your own university or in Taiwan, Hong Kong, Beijing or Shanghai. It is essential to take courses in reading the texts. The situation would be different in East Asia, because perhaps the students would already have some backgrounds.

The other thing that I would say to American and European students is, if you must choose a Ph.D. field, it is better if you choose a Ph.D. in philosophy. You may have to look for a university that offers it. But it is best if you choose this way. A future audience of philosophers would be open and not prejudiced against you. And I think you would have a bigger audience if you have philosophical training. It is not absolutely necessarily, but if you can choose, that would be my preference. If you cannot choose, then remember that there are plenty of jobs available in the departments of Asian languages and cultures, of history, or of religion, where you can continue to practice the study of Chinese philosophy. It is just a matter of emphasis and what is practically available.

But you know, in the end, there is another factor which is

not philosophical, not sinological, but it is a third dimension. I am going to deal with this when answering your questions on general issues of methodology. But I am bringing it up here now. It is important for graduate students or young scholars to ask the right humanistic questions. There are plenty of philosophers who do not ask important humanistic questions. They say instead what Donald Davidson's position was on a certain topic, and then they give their critique of Donald Davidson. Their articles are almost always so boring that they would put the outsiders to sleep and cause the audience who come to listen to leave.

Similarly, sinologists, including those who have philosophical training, sometimes do not ask the important question. They will say, in this passage Xunzi says this, but in these passages he says this, but when we look at this commentary, we find this character would be interpreted in this way. And they go on like this, and you find out about matters of sinological concern. But nowhere do they ever ask the big humanistic questions of the *Xunzi.* Firstly, what are the important or major questions facing the advancement of human knowledge? You ask, what does this text do to advance our knowledge? That is the first big question. Secondly, what does this text tell us that is relevant to human joy and suffering?

The first question about the advancement of knowledge probably will involve some relevance to other disciplines, as in how a Chinese text can contribute to other disciplines. For the big problems that human beings in the past and future encounter, I believe in the interrelated nature of knowledge. And as a humanist, I am interested in the importance for human joy and suffering. And these are what I regard as the three dimensions of well educated young students in our field: philosophy, sinology, and an awareness of the importance of humanistic questions.

On Methodology

Liu: The third point is very important.

More and more young scholars come to study Confucianism and Daoism with different backgrounds. In the United States, Laozi, Zhuangzi, Confucius, and Mengzi have been taught in Departments of Philosophy, East Asian Studies, and History. There are different approaches. Somehow it is very good. It is divergent, giving new inspirations to the discipline. But at the same time, even in the Chinese academic circle, we have lost the standard or the common sense of what type of paper is good. According to some "trendy" theories, like postmodernism, pragmatism, popularized hermeneutics, there is no standard or there is no need for any common standards to evaluate a paper or a research. This has caused some confusion or difficulties for professors to give good training to students. What is your response to these phenomena?

Munro: My attitude would be that scholars must be smart enough to recognize trends. These trends come and go. Sometimes there are useful findings that the trends leave behind. But it is very dangerous to commit yourself only to one trend, because if the trend is later found to be weak, then your reputation may go into decline along with the trend. I think that is certainly true of the trend of postmodernism. One trend of postmodernism is following certain French thinkers. It does not accept any general propositions or universals, any universal statements that you can make. They say that so-called universal facts are all dependent on the mental state of the person making them, and as well as on the historical time.

I have a critique of this perspective. It is in *A Chinese Ethics for the New Century,* in my analysis of the book by Lionel Jensen.[12] His position follows the postmodernist perspective to some degree in saying that there is no such a thing as "Confucianism." My chapter is called "Yes,

There Is a Core Confucianism Out There." (It is Chapter 9.) On page 111, I quote Jensen as saying, "Ideology is inscribed in every discourse." Then I say, "This ... is not the case. There are physical facts about the world that are not so inscribed. These include the statement, 'people die'. " That is not related to my psychological attitude nor history ... and "the speed of light is X." And then I go on to show certain common features of Confucianism and of pre-Qin period that are found in almost all civilized societies.

So I do not think a scholar should be afraid of hurting the feelings of the anti-essentialists. There are kinds of standards that we can use to identify what theories are relative to time and place, and what is common to all human societies because our DNA, as everybody knows now, is 99% identical. Not only our DNA, but we all also experience joy and suffering, love, sympathy, empathy, pride, and shame. So I guess that would be my reply.

Liu: Another issue is: When we study Confucius, Mengzi, Laozi or Zhuangzi, we cannot avoid using modern perspectives, terms, theories or frameworks to observe the past. So, Wang Lai is very cautious about that and tries to avoid using obvious Western terms to explain Confucius and Mengzi. I appreciate that kind of awareness. And I do think that we should try to avoid simply using Western terms to define a Confucian term. I think that is right.

There are still general issues. On the other hand, we cannot avoid Western, Westernized, or modernized perspectives when reading ancient Chinese texts. So we try to avoid this thing. So what should we do in general? What is your position for this? Can we really combine the two sides? What did you do in your books?

Munro: There are some ordinary language terms that are probably useful in each culture. And sometimes we get them by combining terms. For example, many Western scholars for these past thirty years have found it useful to combine the words "heart-mind" to describe *xin*. I have never done that myself, but I find it a useful innovation. So, if an innovation seems to be richer than what was there before, I would encourage people to use it.

The thing I would like to stay away from is technical terminology that is exclusive to one school or one figure. I think it is very unhelpful to take a technical term out of Kant, for example, and insist that other people use that German term, and insert the German terms always into the English or Chinese version. I would encourage people try to find some terms that are generally acceptable and understood in the local language and use them. However, I have not thought of this matter enough. I would certainly welcome hearing what you have to say about that.

Liu: I think what you did is based on texts, and then you found out their relevance to modern society, rather than the other way around. Because Western philosophy is concerned with the self, some philosophers try to find out the concept of the self in Chinese texts. And when Western philosophy emphasizes autonomy, some philosophers try to find out the concept of autonomy in Chinese texts. What you did is totally different from these philosophers.

Munro: I always try to anchor everything in the texts. And there is the first teaching to all my students: Go to the texts, and only then develop a hypothesis. Don't bring in a hypothesis or bring something extraneous from other schools into it. But I do think the social history of cultures helps us to understand differences of perspective, and I think it is very important for philosophers to be aware of those.

For example, somebody who reads works in the Platonic tradition will find that people in that tradition elevate pure thinking. They elevated it above emotions. There is a social reason why this happened. It is that the people who were doing that thinking and writing were members of the upper class that did not use their hands, and they considered using the hands as inferior, as something that the lower class did. So something connected with handwork and with the body was treated as lower in value that purely intellectual thinking. In presenting that position, they were making a terrible psychological error. They were claiming that there can be pure reasoning apart from the physical self, including the emotions. This is factually incorrect as we now know, because we have brain images of people doing reasoning, and there are always emotional parts of the brain functioning at the same time. They are connected in the same neural circuitry. It is useful to know what social class the philosophers came from. And this class division applies to later Platonists too. They became part of the feudal clergy and nobility. In China, it is a rather different situation. Not all scholars were large landowners. So people in the legacy of philosophical Confucianism may not be opposed to hand labor or the emotions the way that the Greek aristocracy was. It is useful to be aware of that difference in our cultures.

So that applies to using Plato's terms in explaining Chinese philosophy. I myself do not apply Platonic metaphysics to pre-Qin philosophy, and do not assume that the pre-Qin people thought there is a difference between a transcendental mind and worldly, physical things. They did not do that. So that is not useful.

Liu: I appreciate your research works which are based on the texts. At the same time, I can find their relevance to modern society and modern human beings. I think that is good. I appreciate that very much. That should be the mainstream in Chinese philosophical studies. But I wonder how one can defend it. Someone may argue that this is not a philosophical approach to emphasize the relevance of traditional texts to modern society and the well-being of humankind. They think this is an approach for historians, not philosophers.

Munro: I will give you a partial explanation to it. I think Western philosophy (excluding the positivistic movements in the 1930s and their modern descendents), has generally been synthetic, drawing information from a variety of fields and then asking the big philosophical questions, and using the evidence from all those fields to try to give the best possible answers. So I would refer to our long legacy of doing that. In drawing such information, we are not doing anything strange; we are doing what philosophers have done for centuries.

Second, we can ask better questions of the modern information if we know something about how people have dealt with similar issues in the past. Filiality is not a value or a concept widely discussed in the West. But perhaps Westerners can ask why this has been prominent for 2,500 years in China. Maybe traditional Chinese thinkers discovered something interesting about social relationships. Then later scholars can use that information to ask questions of the new biological material. That would help us formulate better questions. One such question might be: Does a group derive any strength from the fact that individuals keep track of who their kinfolk are through honoring elders or deceased ancestors?

And finally I would refer to my comment that not all our knowledge is new. We may find important evidence, important hypotheses in the past. One example I used in my book *A Chinese Ethics for the New Century* is the long history in China of the idea of learning through imitation. In the West we did not focus on learning through imitation until probably the 1970s. China has a 2,500 year history of talking about it, about the usefulness of establishing positive and negative models. Because such models are concrete, people can identify with them. They could be used in teaching. So if you pay no attention to the early materials, you would lose the insights about learning through imitation. And I must say, on that point, that the recent discovery of "mirror neurons" by the Italian brain scientists give the scientific bases for learning through imitation. So you combine new sciences with ancient examples and discoveries.

Liu: So, a similar question is that some scholars are pursuing historical truth and objective investigation but others prefer modern interpretation. I think that the term "modern explanation" is quite vague. It covers a lot of ideas, approaches, and new constructions of ancient thoughts. Do you think that these two different orientations can be mixed or combined?

Within the Chinese tradition, thinkers like Zhu Xi combined faithful studies of Confucius, Mengzi, *Daxue* and *Zhongyong* with Cheng Yi's interpretation of *Si Shu*. He worked for four years to complete the *Si Shu Jizhu*. He was supposed to be faithful to Confucius and Mengzi; but it is actually a textbook for Neo-Confucianism. It is the tradition or the mainstream in imperial China. They use commentary or interpretation as a basic form for new ideas. But how do you evaluate this kind of tradition as against the modern academic background of philosophical development?

Munro: My general approach is to be open and tolerant. I want to see what people have to say and not have a bias in advance either in favor of traditional interpretations or in favor of some modern interpretations. I have to read what they would have to say. So that is my main answer to your question: To be open and tolerant until we read what they would say.

In terms of Zhu Xi, I am very aware of the bias of his own philosophical school. I said that because my tutor, Liu Yuyun, was trained by Kang Youwei. He identified himself with the Hanxue School and insisted that we skip over Song-Ming. That was my tutor! So I am aware of people saying Song-Ming texts do not contain the ideas of the original classics. For me, I did Zhu Xi's studies because I thought Zhu had new things to say, and he also had some generally insightful interpretations. So I disagree with my teacher that there is nothing useful in Zhu Xi's commentaries.

Liu: Yes, in terms of the evaluation of Zhu Xi, I would agree with you. I am thinking of the contributions of Guo Xiang and Wang Bi. My concern is that this tradition, or this method, is quite different from the modern academic standard. For a modern academic study, you should be faithful to the object of your research. So Guo Xiang's and Zhu Xi's method is probably not ... how to say ... it is difficult to be justified according to the modern academic standard [using old text to justify some new ideas or interpretations—Munro]. If modern young scholars just want to say something, and they quote from Zhu Xi, Zhuangzi or Laozi, it seems that they are mixing their own ideas with the thought in the classics. If they have to provide some justification from Zhu Xi and Guo Xiang, that would go against the modern standard. What do you think about that?

Munro: I cannot answer in a general way. I would have to see a specific Zhu Xi interpretation. I would have to put it beside modern interpretations. I would want to see whether it is a bias or whether it gives me new information I do not know about before. I cannot determine that in a general way in advance. But I have to be aware what Zhu Xi's biases are.

Liu: According to what you have said, may I take your position in the following way, namely either way is alright, but the approach itself is not a reason for judging it as good or bad, it depends on what you do and we need to work it out piece by piece?

Munro: Exactly.

Liu: That means we have another standard to evaluate a work of interpretation. Could you say more about this?

Munro: We need to go to the existing commentaries or interpretations from the West or to new evidence. I regard new evidence as the job of some scholars who come in looking at new textual sources, such as your work on Ma Wang Dui texts. That is what I did when I went to the *jiaguwen* (oracle bones) and *jinwen* (bronze inscriptions) to find new evidence about the earliest philosophical concepts. So I put all of those things side by side and looked at them. But I had no idea when I started to read the *jinwen* materials about where I would find, for example, the early forms of *de* (virtue). When I started out, I used the Arthur Waley's interpretation of *de* as magical power. It was only after I read the *jinwen* that I developed the hypothesis that I worked out in the first book. So everything depends on gathering resources and then formulating a hypothesis. I did not mention this when we are talking about what kind of questions to ask if you are a young scholar. You must also ask a question the answer to which involves available resources or new resources that you could identify. It does not do any good to raise a question if there is no material that would help answering it. That leads to unpromising speculation.

Liu: The last part of our interview is about your recent political activities. I wonder if you can say something about how you shifted your interests into political activities.

Munro: It is not a "shift." I spent a lot of time on these activities, especially in 2006. I approve of the idea *zhi xing heyi* (unifying knowledge and action). I have been inspired by a lot of Chinese figures who exemplified that, including the people who criticized imperial policies and got beaten. I am uncomfortable with only reading books, talking, and writing books. In the past I have done a citizen's normal duty, such as voting. I contribute to candidates that I support. But the circumstances in my country got bad, especially the fact that the Administration, including the President, violated almost every ethical principle that I prize. Then I was motivated to act.

But there was also an intellectual issue that motivated

me. In my own country, the standard for judging whether a policy is good or bad, whether a new policy should be adopted or not, whether a company, a family or a person is successful or not, is almost always how much money they did make. It is always the economic standard of monetary profit or loss. And when I listen to these people and read what they would have to say, I think they have a psychologically incorrect view of what human beings are. They assume that people are all motivated exclusively by greed, by self-interest for material goods. I think that is factually incorrect. People are also made motivated by devotion to family and responsibility for family, they are motivated by devotion to community and responsibility to community, and many often have powerful feelings of sympathy and empathy as well as an interest in profit. So psychologically speaking, that position is at fault.

When a major policy is being considered, there is usually an ethical principle involved, even if advocates or opponents of the policy are unaware of what it is. And any proposal for a policy can only be strengthened if we can talk about the ethical principle that is involved, and not only money or profit/loss. So it was a matter of trying to strengthen the positions of the people running against a serving administration. That was my short-term, immediate goal.

And in the long term, I am trying to get the general public to expect candidates to be able to say what their ethical principles are, and to justify them to the voters; trying to teach the voters that they should expect to hear from the candidates what the ethical principles are here. There were some daily examples, some questions that came up in my state. In the past there was pollution of the water because of mercury being released into it. And it caused permanent damage to the bodies of young people. And the topic came up, whether the state should take the initiative in cleaning up the mercury. The discussions always went in the direction of whether or not we can afford to do it, whether we can pay the money. Rather, what they should have been talking about is: "Look! The lives of people are of equal worth, and that includes the lives of us today and our children and grandchildren. Part of our lives is our health. This is an ethical issue. So if you raise the question of the equal worth of human lives, and our health is part of our lives, then you should ask, whether the mercury is going to have an affect on people's health now and in the future. That changes the argument. It says, "It is so important. Maybe we have to find the money," rather than whether there is money in the bank right now. That is the kind of thing that I and my group are trying to do. And that is why I am engaged in that.

Liu: I know that you have played a leading role in the Interfaith Partnership for Political Action (IPPA). May you introduce the organization to us briefly?

Munro: The organization is called the Interfaith Partnership for Political Action. The phrase "interfaith" sounds like it is a religious organization. It is not a religious organization. That phrase was chosen because the founders were all born into different religious traditions or secular ethical traditions. We have Moslems, several Hindus, Catholic Christians, Protestant Christians, non-religious people, atheists, and so forth. So the point was to say this: People of a variety of backgrounds can reach a consensus on what we would call core ethical values. "Interfaith" refers to this variety of backgrounds. And in the statements that we prepared we listed the core values on which we could agree. It took us three months of discussions to agree. We can use those core ethical positions to justify certain policies and object to the others.

In 2006, we traveled all over the state of Michigan, holding town meetings, in order to try to interest other voters to accept our approach. And we have had connections with leading figures in Washington.

Liu: Here, in the IPPA document, among the faiths and

spiritual traditions represented, there are Daoism and Confucianism. Does it mean you?

Munro: That means me. Both Daoism and Confucianism are there because, along with other influences, my perspective combines elements from both.

Liu: Finally, this is really the last question. What is the general plan of your life, your research, your political activities, your family life, or anything you would like say? Please let us know more about your future.

Munro: In terms of the immediate future, I must put in final form some of the materials I have presented here in the Chinese University. Beyond that, I am going to cultivate *biguan* (live in hermitage), *kongxin* (empty mind), because my mind needs to be empty for a while. It has been too full of academic research and writing, and politics. I need to empty it. And my wife and my daughter have insisted that I do that for my own health, and I obey them.

In the long term, I will always keep a powerful interest in the question of what human nature is, and what different cultures can contribute on this. There is so much new information coming from the neurosciences, psychology, biology, and other sciences with implications for the questions raised in the humanities, that I will try to keep informed. There is much information for philosophers who are not biased to ask the right questions, because some of the scientists themselves may never ask the questions that philosophers do. They are concerned more with how many mosquitoes have this or that trait. There is plenty for others to do, but I am going to spend more time with my family, and always more time with the *daziran* (nature) which I love and with which I feel I am a part.

Liu: I wish you a good health and an enjoyable family life!

Munro: Thank you. I want to repeat how grateful I am to the Chinese University and the Philosophy Department, and to my close friends for inviting me here and giving me an opportunity to learn, and to new friends in the office who have been so helpful and so warm.

Liu: We are fortunate to have you here as our guest.

Munro: Thank you.

(transcribed by Lo Kwun-lam, edited by Esther Tsang)

Notes

PREFACE

1. Robert A. G. Monks, *Corpocracy: How CEOs and the Business Roundtable Hijacked the World's Greatest Wealth Machine — And How to Get It Back* (New York: John Wiley and Sons, 2007).
2. Thomas L. Friedman, "The Power of Green," *The New York Times Magazine,* April 15, 2007, p. 50.

PART ONE

1. Randolph M. Nesse, "Runaway Social Selection for Displays of Partner Value and Altruism," *Biological Theory,* 2.2 (2007), p. 5.
2. Steven Pinker, *The Blank Slate: The Modern Denial of Human Nature* (New York: Viking, 2002), p. 164.
3. Edward O. Wilson, *Consilience: The Unity of Knowledge* (New York: Knopf, 1998), pp. 168–169.
4. Jonathan Glover, *Humanity: A Moral History of the Twentieth Century* (New Haven, CT: Yale University Press, 2000), p. 142; E. O. Wilson, p. 171.
5. Glover, p. 146.
6. Donald J. Munro, *A Chinese Ethics for the New Century: The Ch'ien Mu Lectures in History and Culture, and Other Essays on Science and Confucian Ethics* (Hong Kong: The Chinese University Press, 2005), pp. 81–82.
7. Glover, pp. 220, 407.
8. Nesse, p. 7.
9. Ibid.
10. Pinker, p. 164.
11. John Stuart Mill, *Utilitarianism* (1863), ch. 3.
12. Antonio Damasio, *Looking for Spinoza: Joy, Sorrow, and the Feeling Brain* (New York: Harcourt, 2003), pp. 167, 173.
13. James Q. Wilson, *The Moral Sense* (New York: The Free Press, 1993), pp. 37–38; John M. Doris and Stephen P. Stich, "As a Matter of Fact: Empirical Perspectives on Ethics," in Frank Jackson and Michael Smith, ed., *The Oxford Handbook of Contemporary Philosophy* (Oxford: Oxford University Press, 2005), p. 129.

14. Marc D. Hauser, *Moral Minds: How Nature Designed Our Universal Sense of Right and Wrong* (New York: Ecco, 2006), p. 133.
15. Ibid., p. 424.
16. Ibid., pp. 112–121.
17. Chad Hansen, personal correspondence, December 8, 2006.
18. Peter Singer, "What Should a Billionaire Give—and What Should You?" *The New York Times Magazine*, December 17, 2006, pp. 58ff.
19. E. O. Wilson, pp. 164, 169; J. Q. Wilson, p. 18.
20. Elliott Sober and David S. Wilson, *Unto Others: The Evolution and Psychology of Unselfish Behavior* (Cambridge, MA: Harvard University Press, 1998), p. 201.
21. Damasio, pp. 111–113.
22. Robert Trivers, "The Evolution of Reciprocal Altruism," *Quarterly Review of Biology*, 46 (1971), p. 48.
23. Sober and Wilson, p. 201.
24. G. Rizzolatti, L. Fogassi, and V. Gallese, "Mirrors in the Mind," *Scientific American*, November 2006, pp. 59–60. A summary of the implications for autism is in Vilayanur S. Ramachandran and Lindsay M. Oberman, "Broken Mirrors: A Theory of Autism," *Scientific American*, November 2006, pp. 63–69.
25. Damasio, p. 173.
26. Hauser, pp. 193, 352; J. Q. Wilson, pp. 29–54.
27. Michael S. Gazzaniga, *The Ethical Brain* (New York: Dana Press, 2005), p. 169.
28. J. Q. Wilson, pp. 56, 60, 65.
29. Hauser, pp. 84, 257, 380.
30. Damasio, p. 80.
31. Rizzolatti et al., pp. 59–60.
32. Hauser, p. 313; also p. 214.
33. Damasio, p. 174.
34. Hauser, pp. 130, 207.
35. Ibid., pp. 53, 248–251.
36. Damasio, pp. 145–146.
37. Hauser, p. 392.
38. Gazzaniga, p. 167; J. Q. Wilson, p. 17.
39. E. O. Wilson, p. 164.
40. Pinker, pp. 167–168.
41. Gazzaniga, p. 171.
42. J. Q. Wilson, pp. 7–8.
43. Doris and Stich, pp. 130–132.
44. Matthew D. Lieberman, "Intuition: A Social Cognitive Neuroscience Approach," *Psychological Bulletin*, 126.1 (2000), pp. 109–112.

45. Gazzaniga, p. 146.
46. Rizzolatti et al., p. 60.
47. Damasio, p. 165.
48. Ibid., pp. 148–149.
49. Pinker, p. 271 and ch. 15.
50. Gazzaniga, p. 167.
51. Pinker, p. 161; Randy Thornhill and Craig T. Palmer, *A Natural History of Rape: Biological Bases of Sexual Coercion* (Cambridge, MA: MIT Press, 2000).
52. J. Q. Wilson, p. 59.
53. Gazzaniga, p. 167.
54. Doris and Stich, p. 135.
55. Daniel M. T. Fessler, "Toward an Understanding of the Universality of Second Order Emotions," in Alexander Laban Hinton, ed., *Biocultural Approaches to the Emotions* (Cambridge: Cambridge University Press, 1999), pp. 75–116.
56. *Liji zhengyi* (Standard edition of the *Book of Rites*; Qing edition), "Tangong," *xia*, ch. 62.
57. David Barboza, "In a Computer Scientist's Fall, China Feels Robbed of Glory," *The New York Times*, May 15, 2006, p. A1, available at: http://www.nytimes.com/2006/05/15/technology/15fraud.html?_r=1&oref=slogin
58. Paolo Santangelo, *Sentimental Education in Chinese History: An Interdisciplinary Textual Research on Ming and Qing Sources* (Leiden: Brill, 2003), p. 417.
59. Kwong-loi Shun, *Mencius and Early Chinese Thought* (Stanford, CA: Stanford University Press, 1997), p. 62.
60. *Analects*, 2.3.
61. Ibid.
62. Olwen Bedford and Kwang-kuo Huang, "Guilt and Shame in Chinese Culture: A Cross Cultural Framework from the Perspective of Morality and Identity," *Journal for the Theory of Social Behavior*, 33.2 (June 2003), pp. 127–144.
63. Allan Gibbard, *Wise Choices, Apt Feelings: A Theory of Normative Judgment* (Cambridge, MA: Harvard University Press, 1990), p. 139; Fessler, point made throughout the essay.
64. Bedford and Huang, p. 129.
65. Gibbard, p. 139.
66. Fessler, section entitled "Cooperation and the Model of Mind."
67. J. Q. Wilson, p. 69.
68. Deepak Malhotra, "Trust and Reciprocity Decisions: The Differing Perspectives of Trustors and Trusted Parties," *Organizational Behavior and Human Decision Processes*, 94 (2004), pp. 61–73, quoting D. Rousseau et al.
69. New York: Global Scholarly Publications, 2005.

70. *Daxue*, 6.1; *Mencius*, 4A.12.
71. Malhotra, p. 3.
72. Ibid., p. 26.
73. Paul J. Zak, "Neuroeconomics," *The Royal Society, Philosophical Transactions*, 359 (2004), pp. 1742–1744.
74. Randolph M. Nesse, "Natural Selection and the Capacity for Subjective Commitment," in Randolph M. Nesse, ed., *Evolution and the Capacity for Commitment* (New York: Russell Sage Foundation, 2001), p. 30.
75. For example, see Richard Dawkins, *The Selfish Gene* (New York: Oxford University Press, 1999), p. 60.
76. Pinker, pp. 159–170.
77. Ibid., p. 164.
78. Matt Ridley, *Nature via Nurture: Genes, Experience and What Makes Us Human* (London: Fourth Estate, 2003), p. 130 (a paperback version was published in 2003 under the title *The Agile Gene: How Nature Turns on Nurture*).
79. Pinker, p. 175.
80. Donald J. Munro, *The Concept of Man in Contemporary China* (Ann Arbor: University of Michigan Press, 1977), ch. 3 on "The Malleability of Man"; also Ridley, ch. 7.
81. Ridley, pp. 190–191.
82. Ullica Segerstrale, *Defenders of the Truth: The Battle for Science in the Sociobiology Debate and Beyond* (Oxford: Oxford University Press, 2000), pp. 391–399.

PART TWO

Application One

1. Gregg Easterbrook, "Some Convenient Truths," *The Atlantic Monthly*, September 2006, pp. 29–30.
2. *Mencius*, 7A.3.
3. Cédric Philibert and Jacek Podkanski, "International Energy Technology Collaboration and Climate Mitigation: Case Study 4: Clean Coal Technologies" (Paris: Organization for Economic Cooperation and Development [OECD] of the International Energy Agency [IEA], 2005), p. 18, available at: http://www.oecd.org/dataoecd/22/38/34878689.pdf
4. Keith Bradsher and David Barboza, "Pollution from Chinese Coal Casts a Global Shadow," *The New York Times*, June 11, 2006, available at: http://www.nytimes.com/2006/06/11/business/worldbusiness/11chinacoal.html?_r=1&oref=slogin
5. Jeff Goodell, *Big Coal: The Dirty Secret Behind America's Energy Future* (New York: Houghton Mifflin, 2006), p. 212.
6. Philibert and Podkanski, p. 5.
7. Ibid., pp. 5, 12.

8. Elizabeth Kolbert, "The Climate of Man-III," *The New Yorker*, May 9, 2005, p. 59.
9. Anup Shah, "Climate, Justice, and Equity," available at: http://www.globalissues.org/EnvIssues/GlobalWarming/Justice.asp
10. Arnie Heller, "Locked in Rock: Sequestering Carbon Dioxide Underground," *Science and Technology Review*, May 2005, available at: http://www.llnl.gov/str/May05/Friedmann.html; Jonathan Shaw, "Fueling Our Future," *Harvard Magazine*, May–June 2006, pp. 40–48; citation from Simon Romero, "2 Industry Leaders Bet on Coal but Split on Cleaner Approach," *The New York Times*, May 28, 2006, pp. A1 and A18, available at: http://www.nytimes.com/2006/05/28/business/28coal.html?pagewanted=3
11. Philibert and Podkanski, pp. 10–11, 23; "Asia-Pacific Partnership on Clean Development and Climate, Project Roster, Cleaner Fossil Energy Task Force," Project 15, "Coal Gasification Performance Assessment for Low Emission IGCC Systems," available at: www.asiapacificpartnership.org/CleanerfossilenergyProjects.htm
12. Dale Simbeck, "Cogneration for CO_2 Reduction and Polygeneration for CO_2 Sequestration," paper presented at the First National Conference on Carbon Sequestration, May 2001, p. 10; Philibert and Podkanski, p. 10.
13. Philibert and Podkanski, p. 20.
14. James L. Connaughton, Chairman, White House Council on Environmental Quality, "Cleaner Coal Investment," letter to the editor of *The New York Times*, dated January 13, 2007; published in *The New York Times*, January 17, 2007, available at: http://query.nytimes.com/gst/fullpage.html?res=9506E5DF1130F934A25752C0A9619C8B63
15. Thomas L. Friedman, "A Partner for Mr. Hu," *The New York Times*, November 22, 2006, available at: http://select.nytimes.com/2006/11/22/opinion/22friedman.html?_r=1&oref=slogin
16. Steven R. Weisman, "Fed Chief's Help Enlisted for Trip to Press China," *The New York Times*, November 23, 2006, available at: http://www.nytimes.com/2006/11/23/business/worldbusiness/23trip.html?_r=1
17. "Taming King Coal" (Editorial), *The New York Times*, November 25, 2006, available at: http://www.nytimes.com/2006/11/25/opinion/25sat1.html
18. Josh Fecht, "San Francisco Mayor Proclaims Urban Environment Day," *City Mayors Environment*, May 15, 2005, available at: www.citymayors.com/environment/environment_day.html
19. See Susan Jakes, "Dabbling in Democracy," *Time*, April 16, 2005, available at: http://www.time.com/time/magazine/article/0,9171,501050425-1050191,00.html
20. For the 2003 figure, see *Dialogue* (the official newsletter of the Dui Hua Foundation, San Francisco), 19 (Spring, 2005), p. 3, available at: http://

www.duihua.org/work/publications/nl/nl_pdf/nl_19_2.pdf. For the 2004 figure, see Howard W. French, "Anger in China Rises Over Threat to Environment," *The New York Times*, July 19, 2005, available at: http://www.nytimes.com/2005/07/19/international/asia/19china.html. The 2005 number comes from Joseph Kahn, "Rights Group Urges China to End Curb on Lawyers," *The New York Times*, December 11, 2006, available at: http://www.nytimes.com/2006/12/11/world/asia/11china.html

21. "Friends of the Green Belt Movement North America," March 4, 2005, available at: http://gbmna.org/w.php?id==10
22. Felicity Barringer, "Officials Reach California Deal to Cut Emissions," *The New York Times*, August 31, 2006, pp. A1 and A20, available at: http://www.nytimes.com/2006/08/31/washington/31warming.html
23. Thomas L. Friedman, "The Green Leap Forward," *The New York Times*, November 17, 2006, p. A31, available at: http://select.nytimes.com/2006/11/17/opinion/17friedman.html
24. James Fallows, "Mr. Zhang Builds His Dream Town," *The Atlantic*, March 2007, p. 92.
25. Ibid.
26. Jared M. Diamond, *Collapse: How Societies Choose to Fail or Succeed* (New York: Viking, 2005), ch. 8.
27. George Black and Robin Munro, *Black Hands of Beijing: Lines of Defiance in China's Democracy Movement* (New York: John Wiley, 1993), p. 57.
28. Joseph Kahn, "China Gambles on Big Projects for Its Stability," *The New York Times*, January 13, 2003, pp. A1 and A8, available at: http://query.nytimes.com/gst/fullpage.html?res=9C04E3DF1531F930A25752C0A9659C8B63&sec=&spon=&pagewanted=2
29. *The Reed* (official newsletter of The Weatherhead East Asian Institute, Columbia University), Spring 2004, pp. 6–7.

Application Two

1. Steward R. Sutherland, *Higher Education in Hong Kong: Report of the University Grants Committee* (Hong Kong: University Grants Committee, March 2002), p. 4, cited in Cheung Chan Fai, "Tang Junyi and the Philosophy of 'General Education'," in Wm. Theodore de Bary, *Confucian Tradition and Global Education* (Hong Kong: The Chinese University Press, 2007), p. 63.
2. "China Vows to Overhaul Courts," BBC News, July 8, 2002, available at: http://news.bbc.co.uk/1/hi/world/asia-pacific/2115571.stm
3. "Judges to Be Trained Within 3 Years," June 24, 2004, available at: http://www.china.org.cn/english/government/99394.htm
4. Jerome Cohen, "Law in Political Transitions: Lessons from East Asia and the Road Ahead for China," *Am Cham*, September 2005, p. 22.
5. Professor Whitmore Gray, private remarks, March 2005.

6. Jim Yardley, "Desperate Search for Justice: One Man vs. China," *The New York Times,* November 12, 2005, p. A7, available at: http://www.nytimes.com/2005/11/12/international/asia/12china.html; Joseph Kahn, "Legal Gadfly Bites Hard, and Beijing Slaps Him," *The New York Times,* December 13, 2005, pp. A1 and A16, available at: http://www.nytimes.com/2005/12/13/international/asia/13lawyer.html
7. Cohen, p. 22.
8. Ibid.
9. Dr. Jerome Hill, private remarks, May 2005.
10. See note 20 to Application One.
11. Comments by Judge Timothy H. Gailey of the Panel on Legal Reform in China to the Carnegie Endowment for International Peace, Washington D.C., April 18, 2005. He refers to "the transparency of our system, which has profound affects on public trust and confidence." See also Malcolm Gladwell, *Blink: The Power of Thinking without Thinking* (New York: Little Brown and Co., 2005), p. 119.
12. George P. Fletcher, *Basic Concepts of Legal Thought* (New York: Oxford University Press, 1996), p. 29.
13. Ibid., p. 23.
14. Wan Wei-ying, former Curator of the Asia Library at the University of Michigan, pointed this out to me on August 23, 2005.
15. Deepak Malhotra, "Trust and Reciprocity Decisions: The Differing Perspectives of Trustors and Trusted Parties," *Organizational Behavior and Human Decision Processes,* 94 (2004), pp. 61–73, quoting D. Rousseau, et al.
16. Paul J. Zak, "The Neuroeconomics of Trust," p. 17, Working Paper Series, August 2005, Center for Neuroeconomics Studies, Claremont Graduate University.
17. Malhotra, p. 31.
18. Ibid., p. 30.
19. Daniel M. T. Fessler, "Toward an Understanding of the Universality of Second Order Emotions," in Alexander Laban Hinton, ed., *Biocultural Approaches to the Emotions* (Cambridge: Cambridge University Press, 1999), pp. 75–116. Citation is from the draft, p. 21.
20. Ibid., draft p. 94.
21. Howard W. French, "As Vice Dragnet Recalls Bad Old Days, Chinese Cry Out," *The New York Times,* December 13, 2006, p. A3, available at: http://www.nytimes.com/2006/12/13/world/asia/13prostitutes.html
22. Allan Gibbard, "Guilt, Shame, and Norms," unpublished paper presented in February, 2004 in Ann Arbor, Michigan. Same point made in published form in his *Wise Choices, Apt Feelings: A Theory of Normative Judgment* (Cambridge, MA: Harvard University Press, 1990), p. 128.
23. *Mencius,* 2A.6.

24. Ibid., 4B.33.
25. *Analects,* 2.3.
26. Fessler, pp. 3, 6, 34–35.
27. Paolo Santangelo, *Sentimental Education in Chinese History: An Interdisciplinary Textual Research on Ming and Qing Sources* (Leiden: Brill, 2003), pp. 419–420.
28. *Analects,* 4.2; *Mencius,* 6A.7.
29. Santangelo, p. 432d.
30. Kwong-loi Shun, *Mencius and Early Chinese Thought* (Stanford, CA: Stanford University Press, 1997), p. 59.
31. Jerome Groopman, "A Model Patient," *The New Yorker,* May 2, 2005, p. 52, available at: http://www.newyorker.com/archive/2005/05/02/050502fa_fact

PART THREE

Challenges and Arguments: Interview by Liu Xiaogan

1. Donald J. Munro, *A Chinese Ethics for the New Century: The Ch'ien Mu Lectures in History and Culture, and Other Essays on Science and Confucian Ethics* (Hong Kong: The Chinese University Press, 2005).
2. Richard Dawkins, *The Selfish Gene* (New York: Oxford University Press, 1999), p. 60.
3. New York: Open Court, 1996.
4. In Wang Xianqian, ed., *Xunzi jijie,* "Wang Zhi," p. 104; *Sibu congkan,* 5:12b.
5. Donald J. Munro, *The Concept of Man in Early China* (Stanford, CA: Stanford University Press, 1969).
6. Donald J. Munro, *The Imperial Style of Inquiry in Twentieth-century China: The Emergence of New Approaches* (Ann Arbor: Center for Chinese Studies, University of Michigan, 1996).
7. Donald J. Munro, *Images of Human Nature: A Sung Portrait* (Princeton, NJ: Princeton University Press, 1988).
8. S. M. Ulam, *Adventures of a Mathematician* (New York: Charles Scribner's Sons, 1976), p. 183.
9. Freeman Dyson, "Disturbing the Universe," *The New Yorker,* August 13, 1979, p. 69.
10. Ibid.
11. Edward Slingerland, *Effortless Action: Wu-wei as Conceptual Metaphor and Spiritual Ideal in Early China* (New York: Oxford University Press, 2003).
12. Lionel M. Jensen, *Manufacturing Confucianism: Chinese Traditions and Universal Civilizations* (Durham, NC: Duke University Press, 1997).

Glossary

Aixinjueluo 愛新覺羅
An Yanming 安延明
Baihua 白話
Beijing 北京
biguan 閉關
Cai Yuanpei 蔡元培
changdao 常道
Changsha 長沙
changxin 常心
Chen Lifu 陳立夫
cheng 誠
Cheng Yi 程頤
chengshi 誠實
chengxin 誠信
Cheng-Zhu 程朱
Cheung Chan-fai 張燦輝
chi 恥
Chiang Kai-shek 蔣介石
Chongqing 重慶
Dai Zhen 戴震
Daxue 大學
dayitong 大一統
daziran 大自然
de 德
Dizigui 弟子規
fa 法
fei 非
Feixiang 非相
fen 份
Feng Youlan 馮友蘭
gong 公
Gongyang 公羊
Gu Jiegang 顧頡剛
Guangming Ribao 光明日報
guanxi 關係
Guilin 桂林
guo 國
Guo Xiang 郭象
Guohua 國畫
Guoxue 國學
Guoxue Wang 國學網
Guoxue Yanjiusuo 國學研究所
Guoxue Yuan 國學院
Guoxuere 國學熱
Guoyue 國樂
Han Wudi 漢武帝
Hanxue 漢學
Hu Shi 胡適
Huang Yongyu 黃永玉
Jao Tsung-I 饒宗頤
jiaguwen 甲骨文
Jiang Jieshi 蔣介石
jielai zhi shi 嗟來之食
jingtian 井田
jinwen 金文
Kang Youwei 康有為
kongxin 空心
Kuomintang 國民黨
Kwan Tze-wan 關子尹
Lao Sze-kwang 勞思光
Laozi 老子
Li Du 李杜
lian 臉
Liang Shuming 梁漱溟

liangxin 良心
liangzhi 良知
Liji 禮記
Lin Yusheng 林毓生
Liu Xiang 劉翔
Liu Xiaogan 劉笑敢
Liu Yuyun 劉毓鋆
Ma Wang Dui 馬王堆
Ma-Lie 馬列
Mao Zedong 毛澤東
Meng Dan 孟旦
Mengshi Jiaoyu Jijinhui 孟氏教育基金會
Mengzi 孟子
mianzi 面子
Ming 明
Mou Zongsan 牟宗三
neibu 內部
Qian Mu 錢穆
Qin 秦
qunzhong luxian 群眾路線
ren 仁
Renmin 人民
renshi 認識
renxing 人性
rong 榮
Sanzijing 三字經
Shandong 山東
Shang 商
Shangdi 上帝
Shanghai 上海
shanshu 善書
Shangtian 上天
shendu 慎獨
Shenzhen 深圳
shi 是/實
shifei zhi xin 是非之心
Shun, Kwong-loi 信廣來
Si Shu Jizhu 四書集注
Si Shu 四書
sixiang jiefang 思想解放
Song 宋
Sun Yat-sen 孫逸仙 (孫中山)
Tai Ping 太平
Tang Chun-I 唐君毅
Tang Junyi 唐君毅
tian ren heyi 天人合一
tianjun 天君
Tiantai 天台
Tongliang 銅梁
touming 透明
Tsinghua 清華
tufa shijian 突發事件
Wang Bi 王弼
Wang Fuzhi 王夫之
Wang Lai 王來
Wang Yangming 王陽明
Wang Zhi 王治
wangye 王爺
wei renmin fuwu 為人民服務
Weishi 唯識
weituo 委託
wenyan 文言
wuwei 無為
xiao 孝
xin 心/信
Xinli Xuebao 心理學報
xinren 信任
Xiong Shili 熊十力
xiu 羞
xiuchi 羞恥
xiukui 羞愧
Xunzi 荀子
Yantai 煙台
yi 義
yinshi 隱士
Yu Lei 語類
Yu Ying-shih 余英時
Yu 禹
yuyanxue 語言學
Zhejiang 浙江
zhi xing heyi 知行合一
zhong 中
Zhongyong 中庸

Zhou 周
Zhu Xi 朱熹
Zhuangzi 莊子
zi 字
zizunxin 自尊心
zui 罪
zui'e gan 罪惡感

Index

List of Tang Chun-I Visiting Professors

Klaus Held (Fall 2003)	Professor Emeritus of Philosophy, Bergische Universität GH Wuppertal
Bernhard Waldenfels (Spring 2004)	Professor Emeritus, Institute for Philosophy, Ruhr-Universität Bochum
Elmar Holenstein (Fall 2004)	Professor Emeritus, Swiss Federal Institute of Technology Zurich
William Theodore de Bary (Spring 2005)	John Mitchell Mason Professor Emeritus, Provost Emeritus, Columbia University
David Carr (Fall 2005)	Charles Howard Candler Professor of Philosophy, Emory University
Frank Jackson (Spring 2006)	Director, Research School of Social Sciences, Australian National University
Donald J. Munro (Fall 2006)	Professor Emeritus of Philosophy and of Chinese, University of Michigan
Timothy Williamson (Spring 2007)	Wykeham Professor of Logic, Faculty of Philosophy, University of Oxford
Lao Sze-kwang (Fall 2007)	Professor Emeritus, Department of Philosophy, The Chinese University of Hong Kong; D.Litt. *honoris causa*, The Chinese University of Hong Kong; Academician, Academia Sinica, Taiwan
Rudolf Bernet (Spring 2008)	President, Husserl-Archives; Full Professor, Institute of Philosophy, Katholieke Universiteit Leuven